The **CONFIDENT COLLECTOR**™

2ND EDITION

ANTIQUE AMERICAN FRAMES

The CONFIDENT COLLECTOR™

2ND EDITION

ANTIQUE AMERICAN FRAMES

IDENTIFICATION AND PRICE GUIDE

ELI WILNER
with MERVYN KAUFMAN

AVON BOOKS ◆ NEW YORK

AVON BOOKS, INC.
1350 Avenue of the Americas
New York, New York 10019

Copyright © 1995, 1999 by Eli Wilner and Mervyn Kaufman
Cover photo courtesy of the author.
Frame from the collection of Justine Simoni.
Inside back cover author photo by Ali Elai
Interior design by Rhea Braunstein
The Confident Collector and its logo are trademarked properties
of Avon Books, Inc.
Published by arrangement with the authors
Library of Congress Catalog Card Number: 99-96995
ISBN: 0-380-80221-X
www.avonbooks.com

First Avon Books Trade Paperback Printing: December 1999

AVON TRADEMARK REG. U.S. PAT. OFF. AND IN OTHER
COUNTRIES, MARCA REGISTRADA, HECHO EN U.S.A.

Printed in the U.S.A.

OPM   10   9   8   7   6   5   4   3   2   1

To my father,
Abe Wilner,
my great-uncle,
Michael Zagayski,
and my great-aunt,
Doris Zagayski
who impressed upon me
at an early age
the importance of period picture frames

Acknowledgments

THE author would like to express his thanks, first, to all the museum curators and private collectors who have shown such strong commitment to the period frame and its important place in art history, then to the staff of Eli Wilner & Company: gallery director Suzanne Smeaton for her invaluable research and editorial assistance in fact verification; Luella Adan, gallery manager, for her liaison skills; Kevin Flaherty, senior gallery manager, and Benjamin Wiener, gallery manager, for their line drawings and illustrations, and to Mikel Campbell for his expertise regarding the proper installation of artwork. Further thanks go to Nina R. Gray for reviewing the manuscript, to Ali Elai and Scott Bowron for their expert photography, and to Mervyn Kaufman, my coauthor, for getting down on paper my thoughts and experiences as a frame collector and dealer. A special thanks to my wife, Barbara Brennan, who always is there when the "going gets tough."

Contents

PART FOUR: Trade Secrets

Introduction

AT first glance it was a typical New York City gallery opening: men in dark suits, women in silk dresses and expensive jewelry, trays of wine and moist canapés being passed around by uniformed caterers threading their way through the crowd. All that separated this event from any similar one taking place in an Upper East Side art establishment that evening was the fact that what people had to look at were blanks: naked picture frames hung against white-painted walls.

It was not a joke.

For me, it was recognition of the fact that antique, gilded picture frames had finally come into their own. It was a show, "The Art of the Frame," celebrating my own collection of American frames of the Arts and Crafts period, the years from 1870 to 1920, which saw a dramatic renewal of interest in handcraftsmanship in all of the arts. I was gratified by the turnout at the opening and by the strong interest it implied. My guests seemed to enjoy seeing frames on display almost as much as I did. Moreover, they took the collection seriously.

Five years earlier, many of those nearest and dearest to me had questioned my judgment—and my sanity—when I announced my intention to become a dealer, but ultimately, buying and selling antique frames became my livelihood. Some of the frames on the walls of this gallery, *my* gallery, were priced at $20,000 or more: serious numbers for serious collectors, a far cry from what was being charged when I entered the art world in the late 1970s. At that time I was among a small minority who cared very deeply about vintage American frames. Most people were happy to give them away.

"We've got a bunch of them to get rid of. Want to drop by?" That was a message I heard often during that time, when I was associated with the Shepherd Gallery, a Manhattan firm specializing in nineteenth-century European art. A friend who worked for an art dealer on Madison Avenue would give me a call whenever frames were about to be thrown away. I would hail a cab and retrieve them. Those gallery owners were happy to have me cart the old frames away. Usually they had just purchased art at auction or perhaps had received a shipment from an estate sale. Either way, gallery owners did not want the encumbrance those old frames presented; they knew their clients would much prefer ordering new frames. Most of the discarded items were nineteenth-century American frames that appeared to interest no one.

I acquired two or three frames a week this way. Sometimes I would find them leaning against trash receptacles awaiting the Sanitation Department trucks. Since childhood, I have loved antique frames. A great-uncle of mine, Michael Zagayski, had been a passionate art collector. When he traveled, as he did quite often, he would purchase old frames as well as oil paintings. Sometimes he would direct a dealer to remove the paintings and just ship the frames. Then he would have them cut down to fit other paintings he had bought. He also used his purchases to frame family photographs, old letters, even some of the watercolors I did as a youngster. Uncle Michael did not buy paintings simply because the frames interested him, but the frames were important once he got the pieces home.

For my great-uncle, the process of framing a picture was like claiming it as his own. In this he was certainly not alone. One way any collector overtly declares possession of a painting just acquired is by framing it. He or she makes it personal that way—in effect, joining the artist in the creative act. That is why, traditionally, at least, so many collectors buy artworks at auction and immediately reframe their purchases, no matter what the original frames look like or what condition the frames are in. Mounting pictures in new frames is a way to position them, make them part of the collector's environment, which was what motivated the great framers of the past, the artists and craftsmen who fashioned frames for art. Each felt he was making a statement.

According to Charles S. Moffett, an art historian and curator interviewed for a 1988 issue of *Connoisseur* magazine, "A frame must have enough character to enhance, but not to interfere with, the work's own color, value relationships, and form." My own view is somewhat different. I see a frame more clearly as sculpture, as a handcrafted object that can exist independently of a picture.

From the time my earliest artworks were viewed so adoringly by my family, it seemed all but certain that I was going to be a professional artist. After college and master's studies in painting and fine art, I was ready to follow my chosen course. But as I also had to earn a living, I took a job as a restorer with a New York City painting conservator, Gustav Berger. For a year I cleaned paintings and in-painted, filling in where pigment had faded or chipped off the canvas. I focused my energies on the craft of restoration and strived to master it. Then I began to be involved in frame-making decisions and came to see how collectors regarded the way their acquisitions were presented.

Within a year I realized that restoration was of limited interest and that frames themselves fascinated me deeply. So when I learned that a job was open in the frame department of the Shepherd Gallery, I knew I had to try for it.

Not that I wanted to become a framer. I had decided by then to have a career as an art dealer; becoming a framer was simply putting a foot in the door. I told the gallery owner that I was knowledgeable about frames, and amazingly, I was hired. I had little real experience, but I knew proportion, I knew color, I was aware of scale. My arrangement with Shepherd was a fifty-fifty partnership. I suspect they did not grasp the frame department's potential but felt that growth might be possible if someone would invest enormous energy in it—which I was prepared to do.

When I started acquiring antique American frames, I brought them into the gallery and sold them for $50 to $75 per piece. These were frames I had picked up off the street, of course. At that time a new reproduction frame for a painting would have cost about $200, but some people opted to spend a lesser amount if I could show them an old frame they liked and it fit. These were *un*restored frames, by the way. When I brought them in, I cleaned the dust and grime off with cotton swabs. I never used dust cloths that might rub off some of the patina, but sometimes I would do a little touching up with watercolors to tone down the flaws. Basically I loved old frames the way I found them.

One day a dealer I knew came into Shepherd's and bought several old frames from me. This was a man who had been giving away such frames a year or so earlier. Some of the pieces he bought that day were the very ones he had discarded. He knew that; he recognized them. But he was obviously glad to have them back.

I sensed that change was in the wind. So I began devoting time to visiting frame shops around the city, those dealing in antiques, to find out which ones were selling what. I soon realized that, although sixteenth-, seventeenth-, and eighteenth-century frames were highly regarded in the marketplace, there was little interest in pieces dating from the nineteenth and early twentieth centuries. I could also see American paintings of that vintage beginning to build interest among collectors. I had a feeling that the frames themselves would ultimately be important. It simply did not follow that an old painting could have value and a frame the same age would continue to be practically worthless. I was certain there had to be a positive connection.

I was also eager to test my wings, so nearly everything I did was focused toward breaking out on my own. I began making trips to the Catskill Mountain region, about a three-hour drive north of Manhattan. There I visited antiques dealers in towns like Kingston and Phoenicia, New York. Every shop seemed to have something I wanted. There were always old frames gathering dust in the back, in the basement, in the shed outside, or in the attic upstairs. I paid $5 apiece, sometimes as much as $10. I knew they could be resold in the city for considerably more.

I remember when a member of foreign royalty came into the Shepherd Gallery with his son and paid $800 for an old frame, it was the most I had ever charged! I cannot recall if it was signed, dated, or numbered, but I know it was a twentieth-century example — and a beauty; $800 was a fair price in 1982. Such a frame was worth as much as $15,000 by the year 2000.

At that time only European frames were selling for five figures in New York — seventeenth- and eighteenth-century frames, of course. As it is extremely rare for a frame of either vintage to be found in mint condition today, such examples are usually restored before being put up for sale. My impulse was not to do that. I preferred to dust off my acquisitions and hang them as they were. That way, I knew what was real and what was not. I could tell from the workmanship and detailing of most examples what their potential value might be. I hung as many as I could in the gallery and priced most of them no higher than $400. At the time none of us realized that period frames might be worth much more than reproductions; the prices we set were always well below those of comparable reproduction frames.

Soon I was collecting old frames faster than I could sell them, and my inventory was growing. Since I didn't have room in Shepherd's framing department to display them all, I rented warehouse space on New York's West Side, where I stored about fifty of my finest examples. I refused to touch any of them until I could establish my own business, which I became more and more determined to do. When I finally decided to leave the Shepherd Gallery and gave notice, I moved my infant collection out of the warehouse and into my apartment, a fifth-floor walk-up in the East Seventies.

It was a so-called railroad flat, no more than 350 square feet. I took all my furniture out of the living room so I would have space to see clients, and began hanging and selling my frames there. At that time people buying period frames were interested only in framing pictures. They shopped for frames to go with the art they owned. I worked with a talented frame restorer who had the skill and finesse to cut the frames down, or expand them, to make them fit. We did as much as we could to satisfy each client, considering our relatively modest prices. When I finally sold a frame for $1,000, I felt I had reached a turning point.

At that same time I continued to add to my own collection. My living room was filled with frames; I had more hanging in the kitchen and eventually in the bedroom as well. I replaced my conventional bed with one that folded up into a large wall cabinet, and hung frames in front of that! By the end of my first year in business, galleries that once tossed out old frames were coveting them and buying them from me for $1,000 or more. I remember each transaction as a special landmark. It was hard to believe that anyone who had gladly given a frame away would pay such a sum to get it back.

Nineteenth-century frames are molded rather than carved, their wood bases covered with a layer of composition material that was then either gilded or painted. Because they are prone to decay or can crumble, restoration of these frames has always been difficult, often impossible. Until the 1980s, commercial framers were interested only in selling a product that was prime; thus nineteenth-century frames with their flawed surfaces were considered junk, and that idea persisted until their value ultimately came to be recognized.

Nobody seemed to care about frames made after 1900, however, so I had no trouble acquiring them. An ad in a local Connecticut newspaper would bring several additions to my collection. People were happy to empty their attics. They did not simply give away these "junky" old frames, of course. Sometimes I had to pay as much as fifty dollars for a particularly good one, but I bought almost everything that was offered to me.

It was not long before I had outgrown my apartment. My walls were covered; there were frames placed within frames, double and triple hung. I had frames stored in racks. Everything was orderly, though; everything had its appropriate place. Except me.

One night a frame fell off the wall and struck me on the shoulder as I slept. "That's enough," I said to myself. "That's really enough." I would have to find larger quarters. My landlord had begun to have similar feelings—not about my space but about the fact that I was conducting business in a residential building, that limousines were double-parked in front of the door much of the time, and clients were crowding my fellow tenants on each flight of the narrow stairs. It was either quit the business or find another place to conduct it.

The first day of my search, I found loft space in a building on York Avenue near Eightieth Street. I rented it and moved my frames in. I vowed that the business would not grow anymore; I loved the fact that it was small. I wanted just a few loyal clients and no headaches, but growth came in spite of my good intentions. My staff has remained fairly small, but many more than a few clients have climbed the stairs to my second-floor gallery. What began as a hobby, at best a sideline, has turned into a million-dollar enterprise!

One of my first visitors to the new space was my great-aunt Doris, widow of Michael Zagayski, who had been a role model for me. She took one look at the frames on my walls and said, "Put some mirrors in them—you've got to have mirrors." How misguided, I thought. It would never work. People would laugh. I was not about to put mirrors in any of my frames.

After debating with myself, however, I decided to put a mirror in one frame, so that if Aunt Doris ever came back, I could show her that I *had* taken her suggestion. I hung the framed mirror and liked it immediately, so I framed others. Clients liked them, too. Soon the entire gallery was dotted with mirrors set into my antique frames.

Aunt Doris was right, of course, but the mirror idea did not originate with her. Nor did the notion of frames as objects begin or reside exclusively with Uncle Michael. European collectors had been dealing with frames this way for years: treating smaller ones as important objects in curio cabinets, larger ones as wall sculpture. And, of course, they had been using period frames for some time to surround mirrors.

Eventually I concluded that there are three ways to regard period frames: one, to set off paintings dating from comparable periods; two, to surround mirrors for room enhancement; and three, as objects unto themselves. As frames possess many of the attributes of sculptural reliefs, it is important to be able to walk around them in order to view every aspect. That is how I like to enjoy them—without mirrors, without anything. To me they look beautiful against any surface: brick, stone, fabric, plaster, wallpaper, even flat white paint.

Despite the promise I made to myself not to expand the business beyond my present gallery, I eventually had no choice but to open a restoration studio in Long Island City, just over the Queensboro Bridge from midtown Manhattan. It was a way for me to maintain control of any restoration work being done on the frames I collected and sold.

Today, unique and important frames are increasingly rare. Art dealers feel possessive about their frame acquisitions, and auction houses no longer dispose of old frames routinely. Now that so many of my traditional sources have evaporated, about 90 percent of my stock comes from people's attics: frames that have been abandoned and perhaps forgotten for years, often for generations. Sometimes these frames find their way into country auctions and tag sales. I find I have to look harder than ever to find superior examples, but I have succeeded by developing a connoisseur's eye. It may take me longer nowadays, but I still manage to find what I am looking for.

In the current art market there is a direct correlation between the value of a painting and that of its frame, and as the worth of a painting increases, so does the value of its frame. People who buy a painting in its original frame, or find an important frame to surround a significant purchase, want to look at *that* painting on the wall in *that* frame. They want *that* special experience, and it is not a question of subordinating the frame to the painting. When the right frame is put on a painting and the two are harmonious, a resonance occurs. The two become one; there is no separation.

James McNeill Whistler knew this; so did a great many other artists who designed their own frames. For them, painting and frame merged in the senses to form a single object, as in the early Renaissance when magnificent altarpieces were crafted so that specific paintings could be mounted within them. I am confident that the frames of most altarpieces were more costly than the pictures they enclosed. One of my favorites from that era was a wonderful circular painting by Michelangelo, *The Holy Family*. The equally wonderful tondo, or round, frame created for it was probably more expensive at the time than the work itself.

We study *The Holy Family* in art history classes, but see only the work itself, not the frame. But when we see the painting on display in the Uffizi Gallery, a frame surrounds it, and the two objects cannot be visually separated. I don't think the painting's extraordinary visual impact could be duplicated if another frame were used. When the combination is right, a frame honors a painting. Every Renaissance artist painted a *Madonna and Child*, and every example was framed exquisitely, but art historians rarely consider the frame, though it invariably enhances the beauty of a painting and enriches the viewing experience.

Today, that notion has been advanced a step further, for the antique frame has become so valuable that it *can* be separated from the painting it surrounds, or even the mirror, and it *can* be appreciated for its own independent aesthetic. Frames are rarely shown when slides are projected in art history classes, but I know many young curators and curators-to-be who have vowed that every museum slide, and every slide shown to scholars and students, should include the original frame, whenever possible. As the frame has ennobled the experience of perceiving two-dimensional art, why shouldn't it be studied, appreciated, and collected?

— ELI WILNER
New York, NY

Guide to Price Ranges

THE market for antique American picture frames, virtually non-existent until the early 1980s, has become a multimillion-dollar enterprise. Art dealers, museum curators, and a great many private collectors now recognize, and often revere, the quality and extraordinary craftsmanship of the best surviving examples. They have focused particular interest on frames once ignored though most evident in the marketplace, examples dating from the nineteenth and early twentieth centuries.

According to Virginia V. Van Rees, in "Valuation of Historic American Picture Frames, 1650–1930," her master of valuation thesis completed in 1991, "Expansion of the national economy and accompanying growth in the arts and antiques market through the eighties stimulated the rise in interest in frames." She points out that the American frame market's upward spiral was unaffected by the recession of the late eighties and early nineties, primarily because museums as well as individual art collectors came to resist spending ever larger amounts of money to acquire paintings. Instead, they devoted much of their acquisition budgets to restoring many of the artworks they already owned, and then surrounding them with frames that were as close as possible to the originals that housed them.

That her point has considerable merit is reflected in the fact that the record price for the sale of an American frame was achieved in the late eighties during this otherwise "down" period: $75,000 for a picture frame crafted in about 1910 by Charles Prendergast, brother of painter Maurice Prendergast.

Overall, it would be fair to say that the value of a frame is directly proportional to its value as a surround for a painting. And the more costly the painting that it can enclose—a Thomas Cole, let's say—the more valuable the frame becomes.

A frame might have value on its own as a decorative object, of course, but that would be secondary to its importance as a surround for a major painting. That doesn't mean you must purchase a frame with a particular canvas in mind or with a particular painting mounted in it. If you own or purchase an antique frame, my rule of thumb to determine its potential value is to consider what type of painting—that is, the most expensive type of painting—this frame could accommodate and still look correct. If the frame does not represent the highest level of quality, then it would not be appropriate to use in conjunction with a great or important painting.

If, for example, you determine that your antique frame would beautifully enhance a Frederick Church, Thomas Cole, or Childe Hassam work, it would have far greater value than if it were a frame that you discerned would look good surrounding a print or perhaps a genre painting of horses.

Contrary to what it may seem, this is not a subjective judgment on my part, but an objective one based on knowledge of what the painters themselves originally preferred. If your frame was even roughly comparable to what an artist used or specified in the nineteenth century, it would have commensurate value.

Traditionally, fine art prices fluctuate according to sales results obtained from the major auction houses. In parallel style, the prices for antique picture frames are determined largely by auction sales—but only in Britain and on the Continent, thus only for British and European examples. Frame auctions are conducted there regularly, but in North America they remain a rarity.

Thus it is not possible to indicate *exact* prices for American picture frames of a particular style and vintage because no public sales history exists. Instead, what you will find in the following chapters are plausible *ranges of prices* based on actual sales that have taken place over the past five years or so, or in some cases on actual insurance appraisals that have been issued.

Note that these are *retail* ranges, prices you can expect to confront when buying from an antiques shop or reputable frame dealer. Should you find yourself in the position of selling, rather than buying, a frame, you would find that the dealer's bid would be proportionately less—how much less would depend on that dealer's percentage markup.

Here is a point that I feel should be made about all picture frames, whether dating from the Renaissance or of comparatively recent vintage: Just because an example is old does not necessarily ensure that it is of great value. The specific frames featured here, along with their range of market prices, are superlative examples of each type and style. They are frames that reflect a specific form and are in first-rate condition. But keep in mind that in each decade there were hundreds of variations plus literally thousands of lesser frames being made that do not have lasting value.

Overall, the value of an individual frame is determined by three constants—*size, age,* and *rarity*—and two variables: the *beauty of the design* plus the *condition of the surface.* By examining the back of a frame, a knowledgeable dealer or collector can discern by its color and texture if the wood is old. Also, if a frame is signed and dated by the artisan who made it—which would make it special as well as rare—the back of the frame is where such indicators would be found.

Design may take precedence over condition, but condition is an essential factor. For example, the value of a frame may lie at the low end of the price range if it is evident that the surface has been regilded or repainted. Also, a frame may be worth less if it has been repaired or restored. Such alterations would be evident in the appearance of the joints and would affirm that a frame has been cut down or, less likely, enlarged. Cuts are fairly easy to detect; they were generally made in the center of frame elements rather than in the corners, where ornamentation is likely to exist.

The photographs shown in Parts Two and Three of this book are sterling examples of frames from the nineteenth and early twentieth centuries. Looking at them will give you an idea of the variety of frame styles that were prevalent as well as an indication of the detailing found on the best frames of these eras. In searching for examples, I have strived to illustrate the types of ornamentation described in the text.

Please note that the price ranges I have indicated throughout this guide are for three standard frame sizes: 14 × 20 inches, 24 × 36 inches, and 36 × 48 inches. Other sizes existed, of course, because frames were fashioned to surround various-sized canvases, but you should regard the three standard sizes I have designated as representing small, medium, and large, and the frames you own, purchase, or encounter should fall easily into one of these categories. By the way, my standard measurements are for the *overall* (outside) frame size. In cataloging your own frame collection, no matter how big or small, you should also record the *sight* (opening) size of each frame and the *molding width*.

PART ONE

Gilt-Edged Collectibles

CHAPTER 1

Frame Appeal

THE house, a century-old estate in Lyme, Connecticut, built to resemble an Italian villa, is furnished elegantly in a mixture of period
styles. The decorating is ornate; every detail has been thought out
carefully. There is even a wallpaper designed by William Morris,
one of the founders of the Arts and Crafts Movement in England.
And throughout the house there are paintings its young owners
have been collecting for the past ten years: nineteenth- and early
twentieth-century works, most of American origin.

The paintings are hung salon-style, floor to ceiling, in group-
ings and clusters on virtually every wall. What makes them extraordinary, beyond their visual and monetary worth, is the way
they are displayed: all in pristine antique frames. Meticulous atten-
tion has been paid to size, scale, and proportion, but the true excitement of this collection results from the fact that everything
works together. Touring the house, you are not struck by any one
particular work of art, but by all of it. Simply stated, it resonates.
You feel transported back in time.

The extra dimension here—I have seen it even in collections
more modest than this one—results from the fact that the frames on
the walls have not been subordinated in any way to the art they surround. Instead, they have been treated equally, like partners. For
right along with the furniture, sculpture, drawings, watercolors,
and oil paintings, the antique frames have not simply been bought
but *collected*.

Every painting has been mounted in a frame of the same period and style. Some frames have been used to enclose mirrors—there is a grouping of miniature framed mirrors on easels in the master bath. Other frames have been hung inside one another, like wall sculpture, without paintings or mirrors. In acquiring all these frames, the young Connecticut couple often paid a disproportionate amount of money, even at a time when antique gilded frames could be found for as little as $500. They never based their investment on the musty rule of thumb dictating that a frame should cost only one tenth the price of a piece of art. At one point they paid $8,500 for a frame into which an oil painting worth $5,000 was eventually placed. As serious collectors, they knew that a perfect marriage of art and frame would make the total object worth considerably more and, in the long run, appreciate faster.

This couple and other collectors like them have come to embrace a tradition that extends as far back as the Renaissance, validating the fact that quality frames can be worth as much as, or even more than, the art they surround. Frames treated as simple decorative borders can be traced to ancient Egypt, but they didn't achieve recognition as an independent art form until the fifteenth century in Italy.

In that country, and in that time of glorious cultural reawakening, frame artisans were often paid more than artists. Their compensation was based on the length of time it took to complete a commission and on the cost of materials. In most instances the frame proved more intricate, more challenging, thus more time-consuming to create than the painting. With the price of gold higher than that of paint, the frame craftsman ultimately earned more for his efforts than the painter. It is no wonder, then, that each beautifully rendered frame represents an artistic discipline all its own, a notion that today's growing roster of collectors must keep in mind as frame values escalate.

The Frame Is Born

In Florence, whenever I walk down the twisted streets to reach the Pitti Palace, I pass the artisans' shops where picture frames are being crafted, just as they have been since the fourteenth century. Few original designs are evident; what I generally see, however, reflects a tradition of craftsmanship that has continued unbroken for centuries.

During the Middle Ages, wall decoration was pretty much limited to tapestries and fresco paintings applied directly to wall surfaces. Eventually a separation occurred: Painters began working in their own studios, and paintings had *engaged*, or integral, frames that were actually part of the material nature of the works themselves. Such a frame either protected a painting the way a book is shielded by its cover or was carved from the same piece of wood — the frame constituting the raised edges of a panel after its surface had been hewn and smoothed in preparation for a painter to go to work.

Often the painter and the framemaker were one and the same, but in nearly every instance the frame was designed and completed before the painting itself was executed. Just as panel paintings had wood frames, frescoes were wrapped in stucco or fresco frames, and mosaic wall decorations had mosaic frames. And in the Middle Ages there were miniatures with frames drawn or painted on the same material — an early attempt at creating a boundary between the painted image and its surroundings.

Generally, artists were commissioned to paint by churches and church donors, so it is understandable that the major works of the period were predominantly ecclesiastical. The late Middle Ages saw a proliferation of altarpieces that functioned as sculptural furniture inset with paintings. These altarpieces acted as engaged frames, not so much to protect the artworks they surrounded, but to replicate the styles of the enveloping ecclesiastical architecture.

Thus the prevailing style was the so-called tabernacle frame, which resembled a door or window with an entablature supported by columns or pilasters. The profile of these frames was carved, like the architectural moldings found in churches. Although the use of frames separated the commissioned artwork from the architecture of the church, the frames themselves were like models or miniatures of idealized churches designed to set off and venerate special works of art.

Stylistically, these engaged frames drew upon a classical vocabulary of Greek and Roman architectural motifs that embodied the Renaissance. By the mid-fifteenth century a number of artists had begun to involve the frame in the illusion of the painting itself, creating a seamless unity between the painted subject and its decorative surround. As an example, Luca della Robbia crafted borders of brightly colored foliage and fruits for his glazed terra-cotta altarpieces. And later, in Baroque still lifes, you might see a book, a knife, a piece of fruit, or a drapery fold spilling out of the painting onto the frame. All such efforts enabled the painter's art to free itself from its own restrictive geometry.

Understandably, since frames were originally part of the interior architecture of churches and chapels, architectural motifs continued to dominate frame design. The tabernacle style gave way, late in the fifteenth century, to the far simpler *cassetta* ("little box" in Italian) frame, which derived its name from its raised inner and outer edges, and from its broad, flat center panel, or frieze. The *disengaged*, or wholly separate, frame as we now know it was finally born.

In Italy in the final decades of the fifteenth century, the emphasis gradually shifted from frames to paintings, as frames were being fashioned independently—by furnituremakers, wood carvers, and gilders as well as architects. Paintings came to be surrounded with ornamentation that had its origins in furniture design and room decoration, and many of these examples cost their owners more than the pictures they framed.

Thus a precedent was established half a millennium ago.

European Pantheon

During the sixteenth century the idea of the disengaged picture frame spread from Italy to the outer reaches of Western Europe. Each country adopted the form in a singular way and adapted it according to the prevailing strictures of style and taste. By this time it was no longer just religious subjects that were being painted. Landscapes and portraits were finding favor among artists and patrons alike. Always there remained a distinction between the elegant frames created for altars and the flat, comparatively modest designs of frames for secular art.

The crude, sometimes rough, ornamentation characteristic of Neapolitan frames of that period eventually found its way to Spain. There, silver-leaf decoration appeared, sometimes along with gilded, carved ornamentation. In Flanders and Holland the development of veneer techniques in furnituremaking became part of framemaking, particularly the use of ebony. And the inlay techniques developed for furniture ornamentation were applied to framemaking. Individual frames often had inlays of shell veneer and ivory.

Dutch frames were less overtly ornamented, but some can be identified by their wavy moldings typical of Dutch furniture, for which mechanical devices had been specially created. The seventeenth century saw the rise of the plain varnished wood frame, a style that filled out a bit by 1750 with the arrival of Florentine and Venetian motifs: carved-relief decorations and flowers, masks, emblems, stylized heads, and human figures on a flat frame trim.

English frames show a similar development, but stylistic trends reflect regional differences as well as political changes. French forms gained favor in seventeenth-century England during the Restoration, a logical development since Charles II of England was Louis XIV's first cousin.

In France an almost fanatical interest in art by the royal court stimulated the most fully developed masterpieces of the art of the frame between the reign of Louis XIV and the Age of Napoleon. Where Italian frames had been small-scale architectural creations with notably rough backs, French frames were richly ornamental: leaf and flower designs distinctly separated from the flat liner surrounding each picture. Their basic design, which was fairly uniform, appeared to mediate between the walls of a room and its ceiling. The backs of these frames were splendid examples of fine cabinetmaking.

From paintings made of room and church interiors of the seventeenth century we can piece together a sketchy history of frame styles. Here the artist can be perceived as the unwitting historian, as little other documentation exists. Surviving frames from the sixteenth and seventeenth centuries remain rare—in some cases unique—and virtually priceless.

Framing's Golden Age and After

By the late seventeenth century, Paris had become the center for framemaking. Other, lesser centers flourished, wherever there were acknowledged enclaves of art, conservation, and connoisseurship. By then frame design had separated neatly into two distinct forms: the architectural and the ornamental. One did not supersede the other; they coexisted.

Architectural frames were similar in their simplicity to moldings and to door and window frames. Often they were painted—in colors or to resemble marble—but sometimes just stained to point up the richness of natural wood. What patterns there were tended toward geometrical or architectural motifs. There were no leaf, floral, or curvilinear shapes. The ornamental frames Louis XV commissioned for the Palace of Versailles were symbolic of the period, and of France's dominance as a frame style setter. Encrusted with swirling flower and foliage motifs and set off by sensuous cartouches at each corner and the center of each frame member, these examples were conceived as further enhancements for rooms that were already sumptuously decorated.

Most of the frames of this period that survive today are the highly decorative ones, frames allied less with architecture than with furniture design and other patterned decorative arts. In the eighteenth century these gilded, carved wood frames were unrivaled in their ebullience. With their bulging curves and swirls and high relief, they seemed to fairly burst into a room. The curves were gilded to reflect light in a variety of ways. For the makers of such frames, gilding had less to do with the intrinsic value of gold than with its ability to transform light. The vocabulary of frame ornament had expanded. If easel painting really was the premier art in the centuries following the Renaissance, it was enhanced even more by frames.

European framemaking became an industry in the nineteenth century, with all the accoutrements of mass production. Frame craftsmen drew from four centuries of design to produce an unprecedented variety of forms and motifs. A plasterlike composition material molded into patterns recalling those of earlier periods came to replace carved wood, the molds providing a vocabulary no wood carver could have imagined.

Traditionally it was the patrons' role to arrange for the framing of artworks they had purchased or commissioned. But by the nineteenth century many artists were expressing strong interest in frames and having a lot to say about how their works were mounted—among them America's James McNeill Whistler, who insisted on creating his own frames for the paintings he made as an expatriate artist in Paris. And French impressionists, it seems, were likely to display their art in plain, unornamented frames that were either gilded or painted in various colors. Painters short of funds took battered baroque frames of almost no distinction—those whose gilding had been worn off in patches—and painted them over in bright colors. Photographs taken in 1890s Paris of artists in their studios show that even unfinished paintings were often mounted in glorious frames.

The American Tradition

The first frames to reach American shores accompanied the settlers and explorers who sailed from Europe with their stores, weapons, and artifacts. The frames protected the treasured pictures that were brought along. Because of the men who dared the seas, Dutch, English, French, Portuguese, and Spanish frame styles of the sixteenth and seventeenth centuries became part of the American colonial experience.

Here, framemaking was part of the output of cabinetmakers and the crafters of looking glasses. Earlier European styles drawn from available pattern books were eventually imitated, but because the skills of colonial craftsmen were somewhat limited and virtually the only frame-making tools available to them were chisels and gouges, the frames they turned out tended to be simple, less refined and more crudely executed than their European counterparts. Also imitative were the ornamented gold and silver frames that reflected the new wealth of the colonial mining community.

In her thesis, Virginia V. Van Rees reveals that "as the numbers of local merchants selling frames increased, so did open competition with each other. For example, in 1768 when Robert and Thomas Kennedy opened a print shop in Philadelphia, they offered 'glazed pictures in the present English taste, neatly ornamented with carved and gilt corners and side pieces,' and further claimed that they '. . . make and gild family and picture frames as usual, at as low prices as any persons whatever.' "

Van Rees states, in addition:

> Interestingly, the artists themselves, in this period, began to re-
> alize that it was in their own best interests to become involved
> in the frames for their artworks. . . . By the end of the colonial
> period the spirit of competition had manifested itself, and pic-
> ture frames were widely available from merchants, craftsmen,
> and artists.

According to Carrie Rebora, Ph.D., a curator at the Metropolitan Museum of Art, "The collaboration between craftsman, artists,
and collector resulted in American frame designs that paralleled the
shifts in painting styles as well as changes in architecture and interior design."

Little beyond conjecture survives of the first American examples. However, a vast number of late eighteenth-century American
portraits can still be seen in their original frames. They are distinguished by their simplicity, crafted as they were of moldings sold by
the foot and ornamented with painted or stenciled decoration that
simulated marble or ivory. Among the painted examples you may be
fortunate enough to find today are early trompe l'oeil decoration,
with its three-dimensional painted illusions, which had become
fashionable in the eighteenth century.

A passage in *The Writings of George Washington* documents that,
at least on one occasion, our first president ordered frame molding
by the running foot and expressed concern that his regard for thrift
remain uncompromised. In a May 1797 letter to Clement Biddle,
confirming an order for frame molding, he wrote, "Let it cost one
dollar a foot. I do not want high-price frames."

Patterns and Surfaces

I am rarely able to find a gilded, carved-wood frame — European or
American — that was made in the nineteenth century. The dawn of
the machine age saw the execution of molded frame designs. But in
earlier times a craftsman carved his designs out of wood that was
then coated with a thin layer of *gesso*, a glue-and-chalk binder that
prepared the wood surface for gilding. (In Italy, gypsum was used
traditionally instead of chalk.)

If gold leaf or a color foundation was applied directly to wood, the grain would still show through. Gesso was painted on; then a craftsman applied a thin layer of *bole.* Using this fine-grain, claylike finishing substance enabled the craftsman to create extremely smooth surfaces. Bole could be yellow, red, white, brown, black, or blue—colors that affected the overlay of gilding or silvering by giving it either a warmer or cooler tone.

The difference between American and European frames goes beyond surface treatment, as European frames are more complex and ornate. I can usually ascertain the difference by turning a frame around and noting which joining technique was used. American corner joinery tended to be rather basic, with domestic craftsmen favoring the simple miter joint. This type of joint was made by cutting molding strips on a forty-five-degree angle; each corner was formed by joining two strips together, fastening them with animal glue and square nails, then bonding them by applying pressure in a vise. The splined corner was used on large, elaborately made European frames, though some American artisans also favored it. A spline, which was a small piece of tapered and camphored wood, was inlaid into the molding strips perpendicular to each mitered corner, providing reinforcement and greater rigidity for the frame.

Another common European touch was the lap-jointed corner by which frame elements were connected like the pieces of an interlocking puzzle. Molding strips were cut so that sections overlapped; when the corners were joined together, an extremely sturdy interwoven structural effect could be achieved. Note that the way frame elements were joined has no effect on a frame's market value; what tends to increase a frame's value is the number of molding strips used in its construction. A fairly basic frame composed of four strips joined together may not ever be as valuable as one of more complex construction—with layer upon layer of elements joined together.

Throughout the nineteenth century, molded ornamented composition material, often called *compo,* was the medium of choice to animate picture frames. Not only was its use faster than creating hand-carved designs, but it gave craftsmen greater flexibility, offering choices from an enormous range of possible textured surfaces. Incidentally, you can tell if a frame has molded ornamentation by the way it chips with wear, but even if it is chip-free, you can see telltale fissures in the surface caused by repeated expansion and

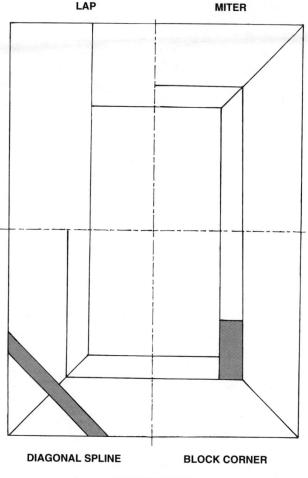

JOINT TYPES

contraction of the wood underneath. Also, molded ornament is more three-dimensional, and the surface has a soft look.

Unlike earlier examples, nineteenth-century frames—once dismissed as junk—are widely available today. They are also highly desirable. The craftsmen and artisans of that era drew upon a wide variety of historical motifs and styles to create wholly original objects. There is an irony here, for in the nineteenth century, artists like Whistler traveled to Europe and absorbed the "new" ideas that ultimately evolved into America's own distinctive approach to framing.

The Arts and Crafts Period

Carved-wood frames experienced a revival in the early twentieth century. In Europe their designs were based on sixteenth- and seventeenth-century patterns, which shared no kinship with the period. In America, adaptations of these earlier European designs demonstrated the fine craftsmanship reflective of a movement that began shortly after the Civil War and lasted for about fifty years. Called the Arts and Crafts Movement, it evolved as a sort of protest against the sweeping industrialization taking place across the Western world. New York frame gallery director Suzanne Smeaton describes it this way:

> The Arts and Crafts Movement placed an increased emphasis on simplicity in design and craftsmanship and a greater role for the decorative and applied arts. . . . In frames this changing perspective is evidenced by the move away from cast ornament and complex frame profiles; what emerged were hand-carved frames with simpler profiles, heightened awareness of gilding processes—which harmonized more directly with the artworks—and the practice of signing and/or dating frames as independent artworks.

Hand-carved frames produced during this period appeared almost sculptural—in contrast with the equally well turned-out molded-ornament frames that predominated. For the buyer then, as for the collector today, the choices were vast, confirming what art critic and educator Margaret Sheffield wrote in her 1988 *Connoisseur* article: "Framing is a mysterious and enigmatic art, its triumphs resting, as in painting, on the unpredictable and the intuitive."

In a July 1990 review of the Metropolitan Museum of Art's exhibition of Italian Renaissance frames, *New York Times* art critic John Russell insisted that "a frame is not just there to make a picture look good. It can have in it elements of painting, architecture, sculpture, furniture, and the decorative arts. It can, in fact, have a subtlety to which many paintings do not aspire."

Russell wrote, in addition, that "it is important to remember that the frame minus the picture could be almost as compelling as the picture minus the frame. Sometimes it can be even more so. . . ."

CHAPTER 2

Elements of Picture Frames

"THE gilded frame, with its bristling halo of sharp-edged radiance, inserts a ribbon of pure splendor between the painting and the unreal world." This was Spanish writer-philosopher José Ortega y Gasset's description, in his 1943 essay "Meditations on the Frame," of the role that frames have traditionally played in displaying art.

The implied subordination of frames to the objects within them was subtly underscored by Richard R. Brettell in his scholarly introduction to the catalog for the first ever, 1986 frames-only exhibition, "The Art of the Edge: European Frames 1300–1900," at the Art Institute of Chicago.

"While we might like to assume that there exists an intimate relationship between frames and pictures," he wrote, "we know that they were, as often as not, distant cousins. . . . Furthermore, one quickly learns that frames have more to do with furniture and architecture than with painting." The fact that frames represent not only a marriage between furniture and architecture, but also a marriage that sets them apart as a separate form of expression, seems to have eluded this scholar, and others as well. In support of this argument is the fact that frame design has followed its own evolutionary course, one that has been affected by disparate movements in art and by other cultural influences that have evolved in similar ways.

You need not be an art historian or doctoral candidate to grasp the intrinsic value of picture frames as a separate form of aesthetic expression. The key to connoisseurship, whether you are discerning value in art, antique furnishings, picture frames, or any other form of collectible, lies in having an educated eye. Often you may have the opportunity to handle an item that interests you, but it is more likely that you will have to make initial judgments based on your own clear vision. To do this effectively you must know what you are looking at—and, even more important, what you are looking *for*.

Where frames are concerned, you will want to assess how the materials, the design, and the finish merge to produce the final product. Whether framemaking is an art or a craft is a topic long debated, but what is indisputable is the fact that a frame is a *structure*, one designed to fulfill a specific purpose. Frames differ in size and finish, in profile and ornamentation, but all are constructed from the same basic components, the result of a handful of similar techniques. As Virginia V. Van Rees points out, "Throughout the six centuries that frames have been in existence as separate entities, the components of frames have remained fairly consistent."

Components and Terminology

The primary element in frame construction is *molding*, which Van Rees describes as "a decorative strip or plane that usually runs parallel to the sides of the frame, often ornately carved." Whether curved, recessed, or relieved, molding is designed to emphasize certain elements of interior architecture. Wherever it is used—around

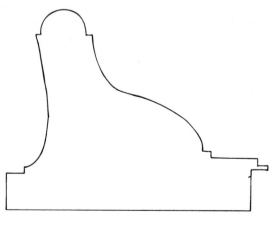

OGEE

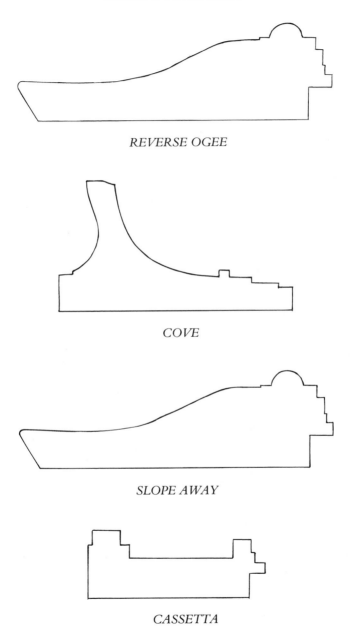

REVERSE OGEE

COVE

SLOPE AWAY

CASSETTA

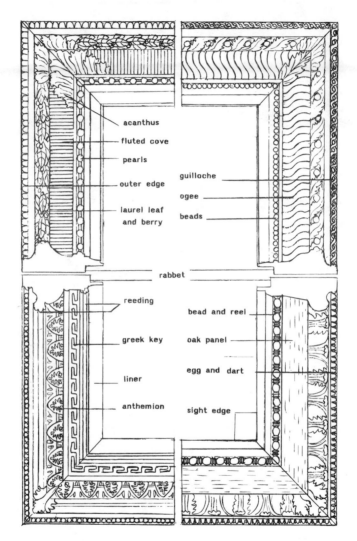

acanthus

fluted cove

pearls

outer edge

guilloche

ogee

laurel leaf
and berry

beads

rabbet

reeding

bead and reel

greek key

oak panel

liner

egg and dart

anthemion

sight edge

windows and doors, at ceiling height or as baseboard trim—architectural molding is present to frame certain elements in a room. No wonder, then, that it is the principal decorative element in the construction of picture frames. The *face* of the molding is its flat or level part; the *profile* is the shape of the molding when viewed from the side.

In contrast to the often stark simplicity of molding strips used in modern framemaking, period frames comprised a series of molding strips. One framed another, starting with the *sight molding*, often called the inner molding, which is that part of the frame closest to the painting. Outward from the sight molding, in order, you will find the *inner molding*, then the *center band*, which Van Rees calls the "center zone of the frame," and finally the *outer molding*.

Different woods were popularly used in different periods and to achieve different effects, but throughout the history of framemaking in America, the choice of wood roughly paralleled the preferences for certain woods in furnituremaking: red pine, white pine, basswood, cypress, mahogany, walnut, tulipwood, and oak.

The nineteenth century saw a more radical departure from traditional frame construction than had occurred at any other time, before or since. Here is how Van Rees describes it:

> As a substitute for the time-consuming and skillful method of hand carving a design into the wood molding for each frame, a form of hard composition material came into use in the early nineteenth century. The composition, or "compo" as it is frequently referred to today, is a mixture of chalk and resins, and was pressed into a carved wood mold, and then was removed and applied to the wood structure of the frame. The same wood could be used for the fabrication of multiple frames.

Through use of this composition material, more frames in the same style could be turned out, but there was one significant drawback: early deterioration. A frame's wood structure tends to shrink and expand with climatic changes, or even radical changes of weather. When the air goes from dry to damp, for example, wood contracts somewhat, but the compo ornament on top of it remains hard and brittle, thus causing fractures in a frame's ornamented surface. Over time, pieces of compo may not only crack but also come loose and fall off. Because compo-ornamented frames tended to deteriorate fairly quickly unless given special care, these frames as a category came to be considered worthless.

My own feeling is that a compo frame in mint condition from the nineteenth or early twentieth century is a valuable rarity, and I am not alone. Frame collectors have now come to appreciate these

latter-day examples of the framemaker's art, and give the best surviving examples the special care they require.

Going for the Gold

Gilding creates a finish that is unique and unduplicatable, whether
on carved wood or molded compo. Except for pairs of frames produced at the same time, I have never seen two gold-leaf frames that
are exactly alike. One reason is that many different types of leaf have
been used in gilding. The costliest and purest gold leaf is *twenty-three-
karat,* whose rich, deep tone will not tarnish when exposed to the air;
eighteen-karat, or lemon gold, is pale yellow, the result of blending
some silver with the gold; *sixteen-karat,* or pale gold, is similar to eighteen-karat but is lighter-colored because of its even higher silver content; *palladium,* a nontarnishing silver-white metal from the platinum
group, has a tone that is deeper than silver leaf; *twelve-karat,* or white
gold, is a blend of equal parts silver and gold that projects only a subtle suggestion of yellow; *silver,* which oxidizes rapidly, looks much
the same as white gold but lacks its lasting impact.

Throughout history, gold leaf has been used to give items of
value permanence and the aura of enhanced beauty. Because of its
high malleability, gold could be pounded into "leaves" so thin that
they seem almost powderlike when touched. Today's gold leaf is
available in 3 ⅜-inch-square "books" made up of leaves that are ap-
proximately $1/250,000$ inch thick. Old-fashioned, traditional hand-
beaten gold leaf was predictably thicker.

Every country in the world has handled the gilding process a
little differently. One way an American frame can be identified pos-
itively is by the color of the bole, or clay, that shows through
beneath the gilding. The bole used by Italian framemakers traditionally has been red. The Germans and British have used gray or
gray-blue; the French, shades of red. In the nineteenth century,
gray and gray-blue were also popular in America, but twentieth-
century frame artisans, perhaps influenced by the Italians, opted for
red bole, which yielded a brighter, hotter surface to complement the
palette of impressionist painters.

Bole actually represents the third layer in the process of producing a gilded frame. The first is the substrate of wood. On top of

it went either a thin layer of gesso or the molded, plasterlike compo ornamentation with a layer of gesso over it. Once the gessoed surface was sanded properly, bole was applied almost like paint. Gold leaf is translucent, so the color of the bole beneath it affects the shade and final appearance of the gilded surface. The gold is then applied in one of two ways:

In *water gilding*, a touch of alcohol mixed with water and animal-hide glue precedes the gold leaf application, and the bole itself needs special preparation. Once the gold has been allowed to dry, however, it can be burnished or rubbed. Traditionally, an animal's tooth was used for burnishing, but today I find that the agate tools made for this purpose are just as effective in producing a bright, reflective surface.

Oil gilding begins when oil-based sizing in liquid form is applied to the bole, then gilding is applied right on top of it. Oil gilding is easier to manage than water gilding, and much faster, but it does not create a reflective surface.

When dry, both water- and oil-gilded surfaces must be coated with a thin layer of protective shellac or lacquer. It is this surface, not the gold leaf, that "turns" or changes color. Over time it absorbs dirt and gradually assumes a warmer tone. Sometimes the surface ages so beautifully that you will not want to touch it; other times it becomes so dark, you cannot see the gold. If you remove the accumulated grime, you risk the possibility of removing lacquer, too, and lacquer is a good defense against the elements.

In assessing the beauty and the effectiveness of any frame, keep in mind what Dr. Carrie Rebora stated while organizing the Metropolitan Museum of Art's first exhibition of American frames in 1990:

A skillfully made, carefully selected frame protects and enhances the work of art it surrounds. . . . A frame is a powerful structure that has a considerable impact on our perception of a painting. . . .

PART TWO

Frames of the Nineteenth Century

CHAPTER 3

1800-1829
Federal Style

FRAME design blossomed at the turn of the nineteenth century. At that time, according to Suzanne Smeaton, two distinct categories emerged in American frames. . .

> one being frames which were created and produced by English-trained craftsmen who drew largely upon English pattern books and frame styles for their inspiration, and the other a much more simplistic and naive treatment of frames, consisting largely of crude wood frames with a little detail, or at best, painted finishes.

The simplest of these frames often set off paintings that, writes Smeaton, were "done by itinerant artists who traveled from village to village painting both the country folk and the American landscape. Many of these frames bear painted finishes simulating the grain of more expensive woods, or simple floral motifs often applied by the use of stencils or carving."

Frames were used both to surround commissioned portraits, the status symbols of that era, and to enclose looking glasses. The latter not only reflected images but also augmented light sources in a room. The flicker and glow of a lantern reflected in one or more looking glasses could create a brightness that might otherwise have been unattainable.

Actual frame styles of this period were simple, marked by a low profile and a flatness that distinguished them from earlier forms.

The finest of these examples were found on portraits and classical landscapes. Gilbert Stuart, John Trumbull, and John Vanderlyn were among the artists whose work was framed in this period's best examples.

So, too, were members of the Peale family of artists. The father, Charles Willson Peale, an officer in the Army of the Revolution and a portrait artist as well, was known for specifying the exact type of frame he wanted to enclose his paintings. Many of the frames he used were crafted by his brother, James, who was a professional framemaker and gilder as well as miniaturist. Two of Charles Willson Peale's sons, artists Raphael and Rembrandt, carried on their father's tradition of frame selection.

An outgrowth of Louis XVI and English Regency frame designs was the Federal frame. Its elements were neoclassical, less detailed than those of the ornate rococo frames that were prevalent earlier. The Federal style in America, as seen in furniture and architectural design, was inspired by a new interest in classical Greece and Rome set in motion in England by the Adam brothers, Scottish architects and designers. A series of archaeological excavations at Pompeii and Herculaneum between 1759 and 1780 had brought renewed use of classical forms and ornament to frame and furniture design. Urns, swags, and columns were everywhere.

Simpler and less ornamented than its neoclassical counterparts in England and Europe, the American Federal frame tended to be light and delicate, with a modest amount of ornamentation: perhaps a classic lamb's-tongue design — a chain of symmetrical half ovals — on the inner molding, an arrangement of balls in the corner, or a twisted-rope design carved and gilded separately, then attached to the cove of the frame.

Some Federal frames included hand-carved motifs that gave enhanced meaning to the paintings they surrounded, many of them patriotic in theme. The most popular motif was the bald eagle, a component of the Great Seal of the United States. Government buildings and museums around the country still display official-looking portraits and landscapes, in oval as well as rectangular frames that were original to the paintings. What has given these frames lasting popularity, beyond their age and the quality of their design, is their representations of native American craftsmanship. They are infinitely more desirable than their English and European counterparts.

Another frame style popular in America during the early nineteenth century was the Maratta style, named after the seventeenth-century Italian painter Carlo Maratta. What characterized Maratta style was a beveled profile and a continuous inner cove design, usually a series of alternating leaves and lambs' tongues.

A distinctive early-nineteenth-century frame design was the Sully frame, a simple form so designated because the American painter Thomas Sully favored it for his artworks, though it is not known whether he himself actually created it. This frame is distinguished by a beveled, angular profile—an angle that could be anywhere from thirty to forty-five degrees. The typical Sully frame, four or five inches wide, had clean, spare lines that would begin taking on ornamentation and embellishment in later decades.

A major change in frame-making technology, as described by Virginia V. Van Rees, pointed the way toward the evolution of the American frame as a unique and special entity:

> After about 1810, carved decoration on picture frames was not commonplace, having been replaced gradually by plaster-cast or cosmopolitan ornaments, both in America and Europe, bringing about what many considered to be a degeneration in handcraftsmanship. Composition material was employed as a faster and more economical method of frame fabrication.

Typical of the new technology—gilded compo over wood—was the French Empire frame, whose American version was popular from 1820 to midcentury, concurrent with a growing fondness for Empire-style furniture and decoration. This frame style typically has a gilded, deeply scored cove and elaborate, low-relief design, with natural ornamentation: flowers, tendrils, cornucopias, palmettes, and occasionally a leaf in the corner of the frame.

There was no hint yet of the flamboyance that was to come.

PRICE LISTINGS

PRICE RANGES

14 × 20 inches:
$9,500–$12,500

24 × 36 inches:
$16,000–$22,000

36 × 48 inches:
$24,000–$32,000

This frame, made between 1810 and 1820, was typical of those used to surround the portraits made by poor itinerant painters and folk artists. Its profile is flat, and the wood "graining" you see was not carved but painted—possibly with a feather instead of a brush—using a spate of colors from yellow to brown. Primitive frames like this one were crafted of various woods, including elm and white pine, and were either splined or lap-jointed: This means the frame elements were abutted at a ninety-degree angle, with interconnections that, like the pieces in a jigsaw puzzle, locked together to make the joints secure.

Courtesy of the Justine Simoni Collection

PRICE RANGES
14 × 20 inches:
$3,500–$5,500

24 × 36 inches:
$6,500–$8,500

36 × 48 inches:
$8,500–$9,500

A frame in this style was typically used in the Federal period to enclose mirrors. Its architectural style employs columns emphasizing verticality, and its gilded surface includes sand-textured areas. The frame was made between 1810 and the 1820s.

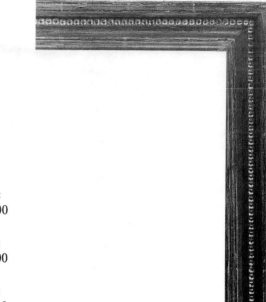

PRICE RANGES

14 × 20 inches:
$11,000–$14,000

24 × 36 inches:
$18,000–$22,000

36 × 48 inches:
$24,000–$35,000

In this detail of a gilded wood frame from the 1820s you can see a handsomely carved inner bead element set into the cove, which is the frame's concave or canted interior molding.

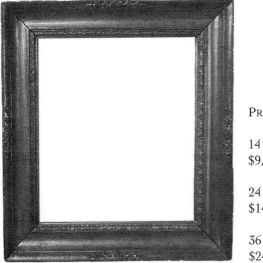

PRICE RANGES

14 × 20 inches:
$9,500–$12,000

24 × 36 inches:
$14,000–$18,000

36 × 48 inches:
$24,000–$32,000

Its mitered joints, which have separated slightly, are evident in this frame from the 1820s or 1830s that was ornamented with applied composition material and then gilded.

PRICE RANGES

14 × 20 inches:
$11,000–$14,000

24 × 36 inches:
$18,000–$28,000

36 × 48 inches:
$30,000–$40,000

Another design typical of the Federal period is this simple, largely undecorated gilded frame with compo ornamentation only in the corners. Made in the 1820s or 1830s, it was likely to have been used to surround a portrait.

Courtesy of the Justine Simoni Collection

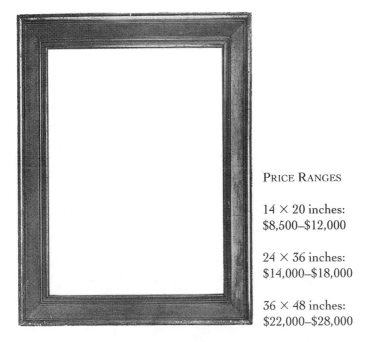

PRICE RANGES

14 × 20 inches:
$8,500–$12,000

24 × 36 inches:
$14,000–$18,000

36 × 48 inches:
$22,000–$28,000

Here is a good example of the basic Sully style, a thick, deeply angled frame that was favored by the artist Thomas Sully for his portraiture. The molding strips are mitered at each corner, and the wood and compo surfaces are gilded. Later Sully frames were enriched with corner shell motifs and narrow cartouches along the outer edges, none of which intruded on the frame's angular simplicity. This particular frame dates from the 1820s.

PRICE RANGES

14 × 20 inches:
$11,000–$14,000

24 × 36 inches:
$18,000–$22,000

36 × 48 inches:
$24,000–$35,000

Although this frame is French, it was not unusual to find American gilded frames, crafted sometime between 1810 and the 1820s, which interpreted a popular French Empire style.

PRICE RANGES

14 × 20 inches:
$18,000–$22,000

24 × 36 inches:
$35,000–$45,000

36 × 48 inches:
$48,000–$55,000

The gilded frame on this Gilbert Stuart portrait of George Washington, made after 1810, was fashioned specifically for the painting it surrounds. Elements reflecting the patriotic achievements of our first president—flags, stars, shields, and an eagle—are among the ornaments, in applied molded composition material, to embellish the frame's design.

CHAPTER 4

1830-1849
European Inspiration

THIS was the era of lushness as well as flamboyance in American frame design. Frames were dense with foliate patterns, and the elements themselves were deeply incised, resulting in more and more generous ornamentation. While artists like Thomas Cole and Asher B. Durand were discovering the American landscape, the frames commissioned to enclose their work echoed recurring themes in their paintings—down to the naturalistic patterns they produced.

It was Thomas Cole who declared, "The frame is the soul of the painting." He preferred designing his own frames, and the ideas he expressed were very heavily influenced by contemporary English forms. Cole's frames were ornamented with molded compo, not carved wood, although carving was part of the process. Production involved these steps: Molds of ornamental design elements were carved in reverse, and composition material was applied to these molds. Next, the compo ornament was removed and glued to the wood substrate of a frame. Fully dry, the whole frame was coated with gesso and bole and then either gilded or silvered, just as any wood frame would be.

Despite the fact that the ornamentation was molded and the wooden molds could be used repeatedly, Cole's and other artist-inspired frames of this period were not crafted in multiples. Quite the opposite. Customers would come to a frame shop (in New York, Boston, or Hartford, Connecticut), examine a great many frames, and select a combination of elements that seemed appropriate for the art they wanted to surround. Because of the existence of these carved-wood molds, it was possible to choose from a whole array of embellishments. And since there were so many choices, it is unlikely that you will ever find two frames that are absolutely identical. To have produced two or more like frames, on commission, would have been a remarkable feat for any framemaker and an extraordinary coincidence.

One reason the nineteenth century has become enormously interesting to frame scholars, I think, is that style could be varied in so many ways—individualized, enhanced, and altered—because ornamentation was applied with molded compo. Some fine frames were still being carved by hand, but only a very few, because of the great expense involved. Mass production meant less time and lower cost, and frames of any kind were expensive luxury items.

For example, a frame in the Thomas Cole style would have cost roughly a quarter of the price of an actual Cole painting. Although the artist himself didn't make the frame, he would have designed it, or chosen it, to surround one of his paintings. Such a frame would be much sought after today because of its elegant proportions. Each frame expressed a beautiful sense of balance between its corner elements and its side panels, making the piece instantly recognizable by any museum curator or frame dealer.

The rococo revival was one of the earliest, and ultimately the most popular, of the eclectic revivals in nineteenth-century America. Its designs, rendered in compo, reflected the earlier hand-carved Italian and French ornament with scrolled floral patterns and foliage. The coves of some frames of the period have crisscross patterns that resemble netting, which was created either by laying an actual net on the compo surface or incising it. I can easily envision an early-nineteenth-century interior with lavishly ornamented gilded frames hanging on the walls along with similarly framed gilded mirrors sparkling beneath gilded cornices, and rooms filled with furniture, textiles, silver, and ceramics that extended the same exuberant motifs throughout the house.

PRICE LISTINGS

PRICE RANGES

14 × 20 inches:
$12,000–$14,000

24 × 36 inches:
$18,000–$24,000

36 × 48 inches:
$28,000–$32,000

Although at first glance this frame seems typical of earlier styles from the 1820s and 1830s, the decorative element that runs along the inner molding near the sight edge is a persuasive clue that the frame was made later, in the 1840s. It is a gilded frame with applied compo ornament.

PRICE RANGES

14 × 20 inches:
$9,500–$12,000

24 × 36 inches:
$18,000–$24,000

36 × 48 inches:
$28,000–$35,000

The increased number of decorative design elements apparent in this frame, as well as its softly curving outer edges, reflects not only the influence of French Louis XV frame styles on domestic craftsmen, but also the rising popularity of paintings that celebrated the untamed American landscape. This example, from the 1830s or 1840s, was ornamented with applied compo, then gilded.

PRICE RANGES

14 × 20 inches:
$14,000–$18,000

24 × 36 inches:
$22,000–$28,000

36 × 48 inches:
$35,000–$45,000

Frames like this one were described as being in the Thomas Cole style, which referred to the type of frame he preferred for his lushly painted landscapes. The inner liner was rather delicately rendered, but the outer element was larger in scale, the Cole influence seen in the curvaceous, swirling leaf pattern and thickly ornamented corners. Dating from the 1830s or 1840s, this frame was ornamented with applied compo and gilded.

PRICE RANGES

14 × 20 inches:
$12,000–$16,000

24 × 36 inches:
$22,000–$28,000

36 × 48 inches:
$30,000–$35,000

Natural forms and the curving sides of Louis XV designs distinguish this frame, made in the 1830s or 1840s. To achieve the textured background, netting was applied to the surface before the bole had dried completely. Gilding was applied as the finishing touch.

PRICE RANGES

14 × 20 inches:
$14,000–$18,000

24 × 36 inches:
$22,000–$28,000

36 × 48 inches:
$35,000–$40,000

Netting was applied to the surface to achieve the textured background of this gilded frame. Made in the 1830s or 1840s, it is ornamented with applied compo.

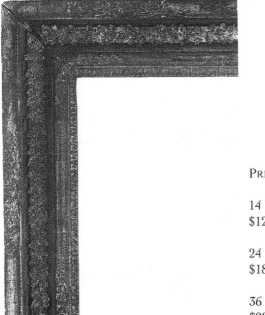

PRICE RANGES

14 × 20 inches:
$12,000–$14,000

24 × 36 inches:
$18,000–$24,000

36 × 48 inches:
$28,000–$32,000

Here is an exceptional example of a frame from the 1830s or 1840s. As you can see in this detail, delicately rendered compo ornamentation was applied to a separate molding strip, which was then attached to the frame in the cove area—to accentuate the frame's own three-dimensionality. Additional compo ornament at the sight edge and outer edge, along with incised patterns throughout, combine to create a design that is truly unique.

PRICE RANGES

14 × 20 inches:
$12,000–$14,000

24 × 36 inches:
$16,000–$22,000

36 × 48 inches:
$24,000–$32,000

Netting applied to the frame surface prior to gilding achieved the textured look that enlivens this narrow frame, which was subtly ornamented in molded compo.

CHAPTER 5

1850–1859
Nature Triumphant

T HE 1850s marked the years when Americans fully recognized the diversity of their country's glorious landscape. That decade, which preceded the start of the Civil War, was an era of exploration, a time of great adventure. Its spirit was reflected in the art of the time, which was dominated by vast, open landscapes.

Western expansion was a movement that had an impact on the art of America as well as the politics, and the art was, in turn, echoed in frame design. The metaphor of the limitless horizon was as evident in the frames of the period as in the paintings. Frames tended to be massive, with rather wide moldings to suggest an even greater sense of depth, and their profiles began to be more complex. A frame from this period might comprise several liners and moldings; there might be two, three, or four sections, each made independently and then joined together.

Not surprisingly, frame design in the 1850s was seen to imitate the naturalistic forms that actually appeared in the paintings. Sand and rock patterns were prevalent during this decade-long embrace of nature, and frame corners were dominated by nut, leaf, and berry motifs that recalled those used in the ornately carved furniture, manufactured by the John Henry Belter Firm in New York, with which American Victorians were filling their already overfurnished rooms.

As the full-blown landscapes of John Frederick Kensett, FitzHugh Lane, and George Caleb Bingham required a complement that was simple as well as distinctive, frame styles became more realistic and less abstract than before. And the decorative elements tended to be executed with absolute precision.

Of course, the Hudson River School of painting was approaching its peak then, with Frederick Edwin Church as its foremost exponent. His landscape paintings remain among the school's truest expressions, and many of the frames that surround them, even today, were of his own design. These drew on neoclassical influences as well as the prevailing desire to exalt Mother Nature, expressed by the appearance of such paeans to nature as leaf, berry, and twig patterns running along the outer edges of the frame.

This was also a time of great variety, when framemakers were beginning to focus on one specific ornamental element to accent a painting, an approach that had become more and more evident since the 1830s and 1840s. There was more experimentation and a little more ornamentation; frame design had become more sophisticated. It is possible to construct a direct link between framemaking and economic growth: with increased wealth in society, there was a bigger market for finer frames. This fact can also be seen in the growing number of frame-making establishments, which produced literally thousands of frames, though not all of uniformly high quality.

One reason that nineteenth-century frames were not taken seriously until recent years was that so many of them were mass-produced. However, it is difficult to find frames of this period in excellent condition because of the fragility of the ornamentation. Only those frames that were handled with great care over the years will have survived with their compo ornament intact. Earlier frames, with less ornamentation and thinner layers of compo, are more likely to have survived intact.

Reviewing the nineteenth century, you find that moving forward from the year 1800, the overall quality of framemaking tends to diminish. Magnificent examples exist from each decade, but it *is* possible to own or obtain a frame from the 1850s that no one will want, even though it is in fine condition.

Similarly, if you were writing about American painting of the period, you would not include the five hundred or so artists whose work never amounted to anything, are not found in the textbooks and catalogs, and do not hang from the walls of major art institutions.

Being old cannot always be equated with being good; what is shown in these pages is the rare exception, not the everyday product.

PRICE LISTINGS

PRICE RANGES

14 × 20 inches:
$14,000–$18,000

24 × 36 inches:
$22,000–$28,000

36 × 48 inches:
$34,000–$40,000

Frame styles do not always fall into decade-long patterns, and this one is clearly a manifestation of the rococo revival, which had begun in the 1840s but was still much in evidence in the 1850s when the frame was actually made. The densely swirled corner ornamentation, shown more clearly close up, was an earmark of mid-nineteenth-century framemaking. All the ornamentation, including the beading on inner and outer edges, is molded compo, and the entire frame is gilded.

Courtesy of the Justine Simoni Collection

PRICE RANGES

14 × 20 inches:
$14,000–$18,000

24 × 36 inches:
$22,000–$28,000

36 × 48 inches:
$34,000–$40,000

Mother Nature is honored in this example, circa 1850, that features an inner spandrel that adds a sweeping curve to the upper sight edges—in effect, changing the compositional nature of whatever painting it surrounded. The vinelike patterns in the cove and corner ornamentation are typical of frames of this period. All the ornamentation is applied compo under a layer of gilding.

PRICE RANGES

14 × 20 inches:
$16,000–$18,000

24 × 36 inches:
$24,000–$35,000

36 × 48 inches:
$38,000–$48,000

Leaf and berry motifs are evident in this gilded, compo-ornamented frame of the 1850s. What makes it special is the sand-textured cove design with ornamentation hand-stenciled right on it. To create the slightly roughened texture, sand or some sort of silica was used, glued down, and then gilded after it had hardened.

PRICE RANGES

14 × 20 inches:
$16,000–$18,000

24 × 36 inches:
$24,000–$35,000

36 × 48 inches:
$38,000–$48,000

Twigs and vine leaves in molded compo are the dominant ornamentation of a circa-1850 gilded frame whose detail is shown here.

PRICE RANGES

14 × 20 inches:
$8,500–$12,000

24 × 36 inches:
$18,000–$22,000

36 × 48 inches:
$24,000–$32,000

This gilded compo-ornamented frame is transitional. Its oval shape as well as the quiltlike pattern that appears in the cove area reflect the 1850s, but the treatment of leaves and berries in the outer moldings, rather than in the corners, places it more legitimately in the early 1860s.

PRICE RANGES

14 × 20 inches:
$9,500–$11,000

24 × 36 inches:
$22,000–$35,000

36 × 48 inches:
$38,000–$50,000

Here is a distinctly ornate example of frame design that spans two eras. The sandlike texture on the cove, with its recurring rock motifs, is an expression of 1850s frame design, but the very realistically articulated leaves and berries on the outer edges place this gilded example in the early 1860s. The stenciled rocks and boulders echoed the natural forms that appeared in wilderness paintings so popular after the mid-nineteenth century.

PRICE RANGES

14 × 20 inches:
$16,000–$18,000

24 × 36 inches:
$22,000–$35,000

36 × 48 inches:
$38,000–$50,000

The stenciled and sand-textured rock pattern in the cove of this frame, seen close up, is typical of early 1850s framemaking, but the cross-straps and the reeded outer edge—all in molded compo—place this gilded frame in the early 1860s.

PRICE RANGES

14 × 20 inches:
$16,000–$18,000

24 × 36 inches:
$22,000–$35,000

36 × 48 inches:
$38,000–$50,000

Rococo corner ornamentation, in molded compo, distinguishes this circa-1850 gilded frame. The long, narrow decoration that creates a ripple pattern along each center band was a forerunner of the fluted coves that would become increasingly popular in the decade to follow.

Courtesy of the Justine Simoni Collection

CHAPTER 6

1860–1869
Neoclassicism in Bloom

THE years immediately following ratification of the Treaty of Appomattox saw the South's gradual, painful return from physical devastation and economic ruin. But in the North and East that period was marked by a soaring accumulation of industrial wealth accompanied by an insatiable need for home furnishings—framed art as well as furniture and accessories. Family portraits produced during these years, plus paintings of home interiors, provide clues to the way pictures were used and hung, particularly in New England. Usually, writes George Szabo in "Frames in America," his chapter-length essay in *The Book of Picture Frames*, by Claus Grimm, "frames were suspended from nails, brass pins, or rods by means of cords and ribbons."

Szabo reports, too, that mass-produced frames were being advertised and marketed by the pioneers of mail-order merchandising. At that time, frame manufacturers were turning out copies of virtually every European style, spreading these cookie-cutter imitations across the country—to small towns and big cities alike. But in certain pockets of excellence, mainly where first-rate original art was produced, the creation of high-quality individual frames still flourished. It was in this arena that the classical influence began to be strongly felt—in architecture and furniture as well as frame design.

Describing the impact of neoclassicism, framing authority Suzanne Smeaton calls it a "formal style . . . characterized by symmetry and restrained ornamental detail, in decided contrast to the shells, arabesques, and scrolls prevalent in rococo interiors and ornament."

The dominance of neoclassical style then meant that the prevailing decorative motifs were drawn from ancient Greek and Roman architecture. The prototypical elements included acanthus leaves, a beaded interior edge, and a continuous laurel-leaf-and-berry outer edge with wrapped corners, which were either mitered or lap-jointed. But the most significant hallmark of neoclassical form was the fluted cove, which, when water-gilded, succeeded in reflecting more light back onto a painting. Some of America's truly great frames were produced in this style; they enhanced the beauty of everything from portraits to landscapes to still lifes. Fluted-cove frames surrounded paintings by Worthington Whittredge and Sanford Robinson Gifford, among others, as well as Frederick Church, whose own frame designs were inspired by motifs he noted during his extensive travels in the Near East.

The neoclassical frame with its fluted cove design is commonly called the Hudson River School frame, as it was used so often to set off landscape art. The parallel lines of the flutes seemed to expand a painting outward, providing a spiritual continuity particularly well suited to deep, open landscapes with a distant horizon line. There was ornamentation, to be sure, but never the fussiness of earlier frame styles.

Another form that emerged in the 1860s (and flowered in America in the 1890s) featured reeded molding: ornamentation that resembled bundles of reeds. It was popularized by James McNeill Whistler in frame designs for his own work. In her 1991 article in *Antiques & Fine Arts* magazine, Suzanne Smeaton made this reflection:

> The use of reeded molding was often combined with another decorative device . . . that involved applying the gold leaf directly to the wood surface without the usual ground layer of gesso; in this way the subtle grain of the wood showed through and allowed for a softer value of gold than the highly burnished and reflective surfaces of conventional water gilding.

Whistler's later frames resembled those designed in the early 1860s by Dante Gabriel Rossetti. The one discernible difference was that Whistler was able to achieve a variety of gilding shades so that his frames repeated, or complemented, the tonalities of the paintings mounted in them.

Reeded molding held its own special spotlight during this decade of framemaking, but it was the fluted cove that truly defined the 1860s American frame. Because of this, its examples are infinitely more valuable than any of the earlier English or French interpretations of neoclassical style. Unknowledgeable or unscrupulous dealers may try, to this day, to pass off French frames in this style as American, but for me the tip-off is the color of the bole that lies beneath the gilding.

Gold is surprisingly translucent, so it is always at least somewhat affected by the color of the bole—a reddish tone on a French frame of the nineteenth century, a gray-blue tone on an American one. Closely examining a frame of this period, you are bound to find at least one area where the gold has rubbed off slightly—from simple wear and tear—and the underlying color is evident.

PRICE LISTINGS

PRICE RANGES

14 × 20 inches:
$16,000–$18,000

24 × 36 inches:
$22,000–$35,000

36 × 48 inches:
$38,000–$55,000

With leaf and berry motifs along the outer edges, a fluted or combed pattern on the cove, and acanthus leaves at its corners, this is a quintessential example of Hudson River School frames, which reached the apogee of popularity in the 1860s, when landscape paintings were so highly sought after. Its complex ornamentation was achieved with molded compo, and the entire frame was gilded.

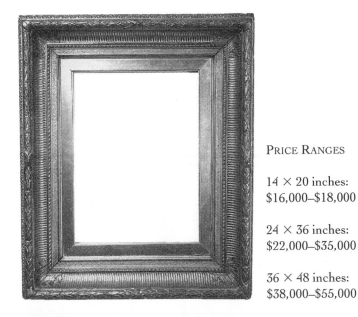

PRICE RANGES

14 × 20 inches:
$16,000–$18,000

24 × 36 inches:
$22,000–$35,000

36 × 48 inches:
$38,000–$55,000

In yet another example of Hudson River School frames, the fluting is even better defined, but an optical illusion takes place. Although the cove may appear to curve outward, it actually curves inward, acting as a transition between the outer and inner frame elements.

PRICE RANGES

14 × 20 inches:
$14,000–$18,000

24 × 36 inches:
$22,000–$35,000

36 × 48 inches:
$35,000–$50,000

The appearance of a hand-stenciled, sand-textured rock pattern near the inner edges, a characteristic of the 1850s, suggests that this gilded compo frame, with its fluted cove elements, was crafted in the very early 1860s. Leaves and berries are dominant along the frame's outer edges.

PRICE RANGES

14 × 20 inches:
$14,000–$18,000

24 × 36 inches:
$22,000–$35,000

36 × 48 inches:
$35,000–$50,000

Despite its fluted coves, this frame's clustered ornamentation at the corners, combined with leaf and berry motifs strewn along the outer edges, place it in the earliest years of the period. The ornamentation is molded compo that has been gilded.

PRICE RANGES

14 × 20 inches:
$16,000–$22,000

24 × 36 inches:
$24,000–$38,000

36 × 48 inches:
$40,000–$58,000

Here is another example from the same period. The combination of fluted coves and reeded outer elements was typical of frames of the early 1860s.

Courtesy of the Justine Simoni Collection

CHAPTER 7

1870-1879
The Emerging American Renaissance

T HE 1870s marked the dawn of the industrial age and saw the growth of great personal fortunes. With the societal focus shifting increasingly toward art and culture, the monied strata of American life leaned more heavily on role models who were the educated, cultured style leaders and on the artists and architects who most effectively influenced changing style.

This decade saw the birth of the American Renaissance, which Suzanne Smeaton describes as a time "when artists, rather than playing the avant-garde role of rebelling against society and the inequalities of wealth, were in fact often part of the elite." As a body, they were no longer feared or dismissed for their seemingly subversive ideas but extolled for setting standards of taste to which other members of the elite responded enthusiastically. Art was no longer outré; interest in art represented a true renaissance.

Frame artisans in this decade tended to display more restraint than their predecessors, making frame decoration more linear, more subdued and contained—in effect, more elegant. Eastman Johnson, a painter of genre scenes and portraiture, and the still-life and landscape artist Martin Johnson Heade were among those whose work was framed in some of the period's best examples.

Looking at frames of the 1870s you would see that the fluting so popular a decade earlier was gradually diminished. It was still appearing, but it eventually assumed a subservient role with respect to other frame elements. Emerging in its place was greater use of decorative motifs on the sight molding, the innermost frame molding. At the same time, the outer molding began to be defined by greater use of running leaf motifs—sometimes naturalistic, sometimes abstract—as well as geometric forms.

Among the picture frames that distinctly reflected this period were the so-called Eastlake frames, after the English architect Charles Eastlake, who authored a handbook on taste in ornament that was widely disseminated. Eastlake was a tastemaker. He did not design the furniture, the architecture, or the picture frames that bore his name, but in the 1870s his name became closely associated with them.

In his dictum on picture frames, as recorded in *Hints on Household Taste and Furniture, Upholstery and Other Details*, Eastlake railed against nineteenth-century frame-making technology: "In place of carving, the wood is overlaid with a species of composition moulded into wretched forms, which pass for ornament as soon as they are gilded."

Eastlake himself was partial to frame design that was simple and that, "while ornamental in itself, shall tend, by dividing the picture from surrounding objects, to confine the eye of the spectator within its limits." His was a conservative viewpoint, one that even dictated that a frame "should slope back from the surface of the picture toward the wall behind and not forward so as to throw a shadow on the picture."

Oddly, despite this tastemaker's concern for "correct form in objects of decorative art," Eastlake frames, though beautifully rendered, have not risen in value as have others of that period. I like to describe them as an undiscovered value; their prices are reasonable and they are also more available—in antiques shops and flea markets.

Generally, American frames of the 1870s are quite valuable, mainly because there was such a wide variety of artists at work then—so many schools of painting and so many great painters. In the auction market today the art of the 1870s brings big prices; the frames of that same period have similarly great value. Even though you may be buying frames separate from the paintings they were commissioned to surround, their prices reflect the fact that the art they relate to has greater value than that of many other periods.

Even if a frame is collected as a result of its own aesthetic excellence, its true value is determined in part by the kind of art it was made to enclose. José Ortega y Gasset articulated the age-old irony of frame design when he pondered that if you "were to reflect upon the paintings you know best, you would find that you cannot recall the frames in which they are set," suggesting that the frame that functions best is the one that does its job quietly.

"We are not used to *seeing* a frame," he continued, "except when it is in the carpenter's shop, bereft of a painting; that is, when the frame is not fulfilling its function, when it's, so to speak, out of a job." Today, the intrinsic beauty of a frame, separate from the art it was made to enclose, has come to be recognized. Being "out of a job" does not impede the continuing rise in value of a quality frame as long as it is possible to establish what kind of art that frame would ideally complement.

PRICE LISTINGS

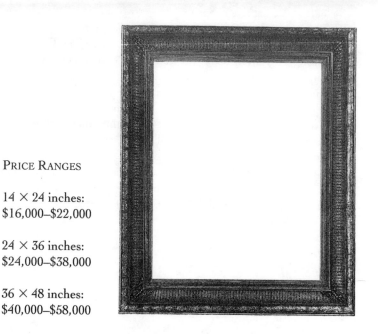

PRICE RANGES

14 × 24 inches:
$16,000–$22,000

24 × 36 inches:
$24,000–$38,000

36 × 48 inches:
$40,000–$58,000

At first glance, this gilded frame recalls the 1860s, but close examination reveals a unique rendering of the cove design as well as an intricately floral outer edge—both the result of applied compo—that place it among frames more typical of the early 1870s.

PRICE RANGES

14 × 20 inches:
$16,000–$22,000

24 × 36 inches:
$24,000–$38,000

36 × 48 inches:
$40,000–$50,000

Geometric motifs were popular in the 1870s, when most patterned ornamentation tended to be structured and contained. Gilded compo frames like this one were used traditionally to enclose paintings of interior scenes as often as landscapes.

PRICE RANGES

14 × 20 inches:
$16,000–$18,000

24 × 36 inches:
$22,000–$35,000

36 × 48 inches:
$35,000–$50,000

An anthemion pattern, a flat floral form typical of relief sculpture, is the dominant decorative motif of this circa-1870 frame, with its sand-textured inner band. To achieve the desired roughness, sand and/or some type of silica was applied to the compo surface before gilding.

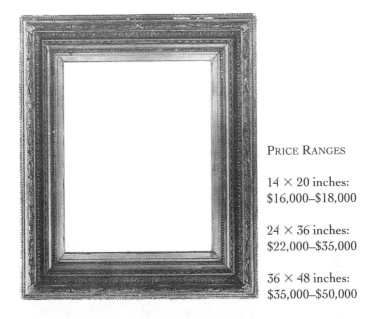

PRICE RANGES

14 × 20 inches:
$16,000–$18,000

24 × 36 inches:
$22,000–$35,000

36 × 48 inches:
$35,000–$50,000

Frame ornamentation began taking on greater complexity and density in the 1870s, and this example was typical. Despite the two-dimensionality of the photograph, you can imagine that this gilded compo frame had a higher profile than most earlier examples.

PRICE RANGES

14 × 20 inches:
$16,000–$18,000

24 × 36 inches:
$22,000–$35,000

36 × 48 inches:
$35,000–$50,000

The flat, floral anthemion pattern resembling a spade shape on the center band of this gilded frame marks it as a prime example of 1870s frame design in applied compo.

PRICE RANGES

14 × 20 inches:
$18,000–$22,000

24 × 36 inches:
$24,000–$38,000

36 × 48 inches:
$40,000–$60,000

Here, in close-up, it is possible to examine the complex and sophisticated geometric decorative ornamentation, in applied composition material, that was typical of gilded frames of the 1870s. With its well-defined patterns and crisp detailing, this frame is an exceptional example.

Courtesy of the Justine Simoni Collection

Price Ranges

14 × 20 inches:
$16,000–$18,000

24 × 36 inches:
$22,000–$35,000

36 × 48 inches:
$35,000–$50,000

Mother Nature was not neglected in the 1870s, as you can see by the leaf and berry motifs on the outer edges of this gilded compo frame and the densely articulated acanthus leaves on the center band.

Price Ranges

14 × 20 inches:
$16,000–$18,000

24 × 36 inches:
$22,000–$35,000

36 × 48 inches:
$35,000–$50,000

Nature is extolled in another typical example of 1870s gilded compo frame design, with an anthemion pattern along the center band and alternating leaves and berries strewn along the outer edge.

Price Ranges

14 × 20 inches:
$3,500–$4,500

24 × 36 inches:
$5,500–$7,500

36 × 48 inches:
$11,000–$12,000

A frame that typifies the simplicity of Eastlake design, this one is marked by a characteristic frame profile that slopes back, away from the picture surface, rather than toward the picture plane, a more conventional nineteenth-century configuration. In the Eastlake tradition of simplicity, the incised decoration within the wood veneer was gilded.

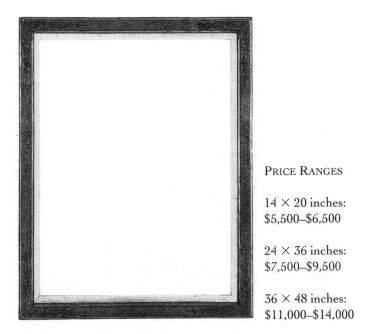

PRICE RANGES

14 × 20 inches:
$5,500–$6,500

24 × 36 inches:
$7,500–$9,500

36 × 48 inches:
$11,000–$14,000

In a striking example of Eastlake design, this frame is burled maple with incised decoration and a gilded inner liner. Generally, in frames of this style, the gilded areas were silvered, then coated with ocher shellac.

PRICE RANGES

14 × 20 inches:
$2,500–$3,500

24 × 36 inches:
$5,500–$7,500

36 × 48 inches:
$7,500–$9,500

In this detail from an Eastlake walnut frame of the 1870s, you can see that the center panel has been coated with black lacquer and the corner decoration has been incised.

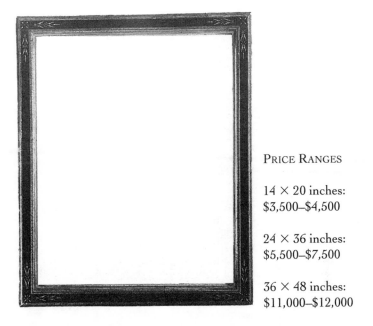

PRICE RANGES

14 × 20 inches:
$3,500–$4,500

24 × 36 inches:
$5,500–$7,500

36 × 48 inches:
$11,000–$12,000

Increased use of applied decorative elements and gilded areas confirms that this Eastlake-style frame is a relatively late example, from either the late 1870s or early 1880s. The center panel is black lacquer with gilded corner decoration; the remainder of the frame is gilded compo.

PRICE RANGES

14 × 20 inches:
$5,500–$6,500

24 × 36 inches:
$7,500–$9,500

36 × 48 inches:
$11,000–$14,000

Although it bears the characteristics of Eastlake style, this silvered frame, with its increased use of compo ornament, is another later example, probably from the early 1880s. A formal arrangement of leaf and vine elements makes up the corner decoration, incised in a black-lacquered outer panel.

PRICE RANGES

14 × 20 inches:
$5,500–$8,500

24 × 36 inches:
$12,000–$18,000

36 × 48 inches:
$18,000–$28,000

Geometric patterns incised in black lacquer distinguish this Eastlake frame from the late 1870s or early 1880s. Ornamentation on the inner and outer bands is gilded composition material.

CHAPTER 8

1880–1889
Era of Opulence

For the most part, the 1880s marked a continuation of many of the framing trends of the previous decade, though with some notable additions. Particularly evident was a broader and more exuberant design vocabulary and the fact that a wider-than-ever variety of forms was being used interchangeably. A single frame might include a whole range of forms, a mixture unlike that seen in early frame design.

Through the study of frames I find it possible to trace aspects of the social history of the period; in the 1880s there is no denying a pervasive and undeniable opulence. Both architecture and design tended to be densely embellished, and domestic interiors were grander and more complex than in previous eras. Many of the most popular frame designs embodied French influence—adaptations of Louis XIII designs, for example, as evidenced in frames inspired by those of the Barbizon School; other frame designs displayed Moorish or Islamic motifs. The brightness of the gilding, far greater than before, was emphasized by highly burnished surfaces, adding another dimension of richness.

Refinement was the hallmark, and the principal tastemaker of the decade was Stanford White. In 1880, upon returning from his first trip to Europe, the architect entered into a significant partnership. The firm McKim, Mead and White would leave its Beaux-Arts–inspired stamp on buildings and monuments countrywide and set a style that would be followed—revered but sometimes reviled—throughout the next century. White's unique vision would flower more fully with the frames he designed in the 1890s.

White's design interests were vast and extended far beyond the rarified realm of architecture, ultimately including jewelry and furniture as well as frame design. Writing in *Antiques & Fine Art* magazine in 1991, Suzanne Smeaton made this observation:

> It is not surprising . . . to see the refined and complex vision White brought to his design of picture frames—an obvious adjunct to his work as an architect and his close friendship with numerous artists. . . . Though White did not make the frames himself, he did create meticulous drawings of their ornamentation and closely supervised their execution by chosen craftsmen.

White's frame designs expressed an identifiably architectural elegance. One of these, the tabernacle style, was inspired by Italian Renaissance frames and architectural ornament. Other designs featured angled profiles that, like Eastlake frames, sloped away from a mounted painting rather than toward it. Abbott Thayer, Thomas Wilmer Dewing, and Augustus Saint-Gaudens numbered among the artist friends for whom Stanford White created frames.

There is nothing marked or imprinted on any frame to identify it as a Stanford White design; true affirmation is purely visual. The delicacy of each design is noteworthy. He used certain proportions that no one else did, and long after his death, frames reproduced in the White style continued to be made and sold. In a 1989 article in *The Magazine Antiques*, Suzanne Smeaton describes White frames as "timeless—a sophisticated blend of classic architectural elements and a unique artistic sensitivity."

White designed both for specific artists, among them his friends, of course, and for specific paintings. He also had a working relationship with a number of top framing establishments that was useful to him. He would direct art collectors to key framers with designs that they, in turn, would execute—and reward him with 15 percent of the sale price. In this arrangement each design was created for a specific painting. He would sometimes vary a design, from one frame to another, but would never permit a framer to resell any of his designs during his lifetime. He offered his clients the choice of either carved or molded-compo ornament, and his gilded carved frames became the most expensive, and valuable, frames of the period.

PRICE LISTINGS

PRICE RANGES

14 × 20 inches:
$18,000–$22,000

24 × 36 inches:
$24,000–$38,000

36 × 48 inches:
$40,000–$60,000

Typical of frames of this period, this one can clearly be seen to comprise two stages. First is a series of flat panels that are intricately decorated: gilded floral designs on compo. Second is a separate mahogany shadow box with incised decoration at the corners.

Courtesy of the Justine Simoni Collection

PRICE RANGES

14 × 20 inches:
$18,000–$22,000

24 × 36 inches:
$24,000–$38,000

36 × 48 inches:
$40,000–$65,000

In this gilded frame of the 1880s, molded compo ornamentation appears only on the three outer bands, or molding strips. The flat inner panels have been decorated with incised rather than applied designs.

PRICE RANGES

14 × 20 inches:
$18,000–$22,000

24 × 36 inches:
$24,000–$38,000

36 × 48 inches:
$40,000–$65,000

Leaf, berry, blossom, and vine motifs are neatly contained in this gilded compo frame of the period. Its luxurious and varied ornament characterizes this as a superlative example.

Courtesy of the Justine Simoni Collection

PRICE RANGES

14 × 20 inches:
$18,000–$22,000

24 × 36 inches:
$24,000–$38,000

36 × 48 inches:
$40,000–$65,000

In this circa-1880 frame, the flat inner panel was sand-textured before the compo was gilded, but the key to its vintage lies in the intricate outer band design made up of a variety of flowers.

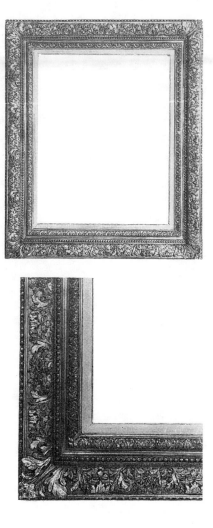

PRICE RANGES

14 × 20 inches:
$16,000–$18,000

24 × 36 inches:
$22,000–$35,000

36 × 48 inches:
$35,000–$45,000

This gilded frame, with its strong convex profile and richly decorated compo surface, is typical of designs inspired by the frames found on French paintings of the Barbizon School.

PRICE RANGES

14 × 20 inches:
$16,000–$18,000

24 × 36 inches:
$22,000–$35,000

36 × 48 inches:
$35,000–$45,000

The Barbizon School frame had many variations. All, like this one, are characterized by a convex frame profile and an effusion of molded-compo floral motifs plus finely detailed design motifs on both the inner and outer elements.

PRICE RANGES

14 × 20 inches:
$16,000–$18,000

24 × 36 inches:
$22,000–$35,000

36 × 48 inches:
$35,000–$45,000

Here is a Barbizon-style gilded frame that encapsulates the major design trends of the nineteenth century. Leaves, flowers, beading, and fluting have been used judiciously, and there is much finely wrought decoration in the molded compo on the inner and outer edges.

PRICE RANGES

14 × 20 inches:
$18,000–$22,000

24 × 36 inches:
$24,000–$38,000

36 × 48 inches:
$40,000–$65,000

Moorish design and Islamic calligraphy were popular decorative motifs in all the decorative arts of the 1880s, frames included. On the back of this gilded compo example is the framemaker's label, "Bigelow & Jordan, Boston."

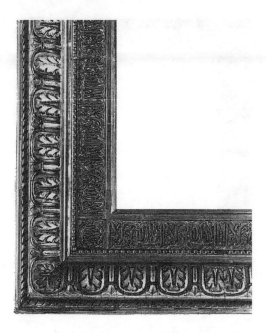

Price Ranges

14 × 20 inches:
$18,000–$22,000

24 × 36 inches:
$24,000–$38,000

36 × 48 inches:
$40,000–$60,000

In this detail from an 1880s gilded frame, you can almost "read" the Islamic calligraphy that comprises the principal decorative element in applied compo.

Courtesy of the Justine Simoni Collection

PRICE RANGES

14 × 20 inches:
$18,000–$22,000

24 × 36 inches:
$24,000–$32,000

36 × 48 inches:
$40,000–$65,000

Leaf and berry motifs along the outer edges were not specific to any one period, but the Islamic-inspired ornamentation of this gilded compo example places it unmistakably in the 1880s.

Courtesy of the Justine Simoni Collection

PRICE RANGES

14 × 20 inches:
$16,000–$18,000

24 × 36 inches:
$20,000–$28,000

36 × 48 inches:
$30,000–$42,000

Intricately rendered applied-compo ornamentation, particularly the generous use of geometric motifs, marks this gilded frame as a fine example of 1880s design. Its mostly flat profile suggests that it was crafted late in the decade.

CHAPTER 9

1890–1899
Artistry versus Mass Production

In the final decade of the nineteenth century, American frame-making began, at last, to come into its own as a separate entity. Various European influences had shaped our domestic approach to frame design. But what emerged in the 1890s, as exemplified by the frames of Stanford White, bore unmistakably American characteristics.

By this decade, picture frames had grown so popular that they were being turned out in rapid order and in such volume that framemaking was no longer the sole preserve of the individual artisan. The demand for quality frames—by museums, galleries, and collectors alike—was met by a growing number of high-quality framing firms, each equipped with large workrooms. As the decade progressed, Boston moved into the forefront of frame design as the home of such important designer-craftsmen as Charles Prendergast, whose brother Maurice was a highly respected painter, and Hermann Dudley Murphy.

Murphy had studied art at the Boston Museum School and considered himself a painter when he sojourned to Paris in the 1890s. There he came under the influence of James McNeill Whistler, whose atelier was credited with bringing a great many young artists together. However, it was not in his painting but in his framemaking that Murphy felt Whistler's profound influence, for Murphy came to concur with Whistler's long-held beliefs that a frame affects the way a work of art is perceived, that a painting and its frame should be compatible in style and color, and that framed art should harmonize with its environment.

Like Whistler, Murphy would sign the frames he designed and crafted, demonstrating his high regard for them as art objects. Ultimately Murphy's ideas would have great impact on framemaking in America, for it would be as a framer that he would achieve success and recognition when he returned from Paris in 1897. Unable to afford the superior frames he felt his work should have, he assembled the tools and honed the skills necessary to make them himself. Within a year, in many a published review of his paintings, he was being praised for surrounding them with frames of special beauty.

By signing and dating his frames, Murphy seemed determined to point up the artistry they expressed, just as he would sign and date the paintings he made, which never quite rivaled his frames in lasting impact or interest. Murphy's frames, like those of his contemporaries, represented a synthesis of styles extending as far back in history as the Renaissance. His designs often resembled those of *cassetta* frames, which featured a flat center panel and raised edges. The carved designs at the outer corners were derived from *sgraffito* decoration of sixteenth-century Venetian frames—in which ornament was created by scratching through applied color to uncover the gold leaf that lay underneath.

Murphy, in turn, encouraged his neighbor Charles Prendergast, a gifted whittler since childhood, to make frames in the mid-1890s. Prendergast's designs drew on many sources. Persian and Chinese art housed in Boston's Museum of Fine Arts figure prominently, as well as the observations he made during his trips to Europe. Soon the demand for Prendergast frames was so great that at times the only way he could fill all his orders was by enlisting his painter-brother's help. Thus some Prendergast frames bore Maurice's as well as Charles's signature. Eventually Prendergast would join Hermann Dudley Murphy in creating one of Boston's most renowned framing establishments.

Another leading firm already achieving prominence then was Foster Brothers, formed in 1875 by John Roy Foster and Stephen Bartlett Foster. Among the Boston painters whose work they mounted were portrait artist William Paxton and the American impressionist Edmund Tarbell. Foster Brothers frames are distinguished by the way they blended rippled moldings and special corner treatments, recalling earlier Dutch frames, with the simple foliate designs more characteristic of American work. Rich gold-leaf gilding matched the masterful hand carving that was the firm's hallmark.

Outside the Boston area, the Newcomb-Macklin Company was established in 1883, when John C. Newcomb and Charles Macklin became partners. Newcomb-Macklin would achieve real prominence in the early 1900s, with showrooms in New York City and Chicago and a brigade of salesmen who fanned out across the country.

What joined many American architects, frame designers, and artists together in a common purpose during the closing years of the nineteenth century was a gradual shift in interest from the Aesthetic Movement to the Arts and Crafts Movement. The Aesthetic Movement had begun in England three decades earlier and gathered force as more and more artists came to revere fine craftsmanship and the use of natural materials. Their focus was surface ornament, however; the Arts and Crafts Movement developed out of concern for form and structure. Both groups shared in the exaltation of fine craftsmanship, but Arts and Crafts adherents eschewed machine production, whereas those in the Aesthetic Movement were caught up in the excitement of it.

Each group had its moment, and each exercised some influence, helping to change the way many people viewed the fruits of mass production. Indeed, the dawn of the twentieth century would see a return to earlier values that not only emphasized craftsmanship but also reflected a firm rejection of sweeping industrialization.

PRICE LISTINGS

PRICE RANGES

14 × 20 inches:
$35,000–$45,000

24 × 36 inches:
$65,000–$95,000

36 × 48 inches:
$125,000–$225,000

Executed by the Newcomb-Macklin Company from a circa-1900 design, this tabernacle-style frame in gilded compo is typical of the frames Stanford White created for many artists, notably the New York painter Abbott Thayer. It is a rare example in pristine condition, thus extremely valuable.

Courtesy of Gold Leaf Studios

PRICE RANGES

14 × 20 inches:
$35,000–$45,000

24 × 36 inches:
$55,000–$95,000

36 × 48 inches:
$125,000–$225,000

Ornate without being fussy, this Stanford White–designed gilded frame from the 1890s has an inner band whose smooth, clean surface was crafted to reflect light onto whatever painting was enclosed. The ornamentation was applied composition material.

Private collection

PRICE RANGES

14 × 20 inches:
$35,000–$40,000

24 × 36 inches:
$50,000–$85,000

36 × 48 inches:
$125,000–$185,000

A highly detailed grill pattern is evident in this design, which is typical of the gilded frames Stanford White created for the portrait and figurative artist Thomas Wilmer Dewing in the 1890s. In a contrasting detail, lotus-blossom motifs in applied compo travel the entire perimeter of one inner band.

PRICE RANGES

14 × 20 inches:
$18,000–$25,000

24 × 36 inches:
$35,000–$45,000

36 × 48 inches:
$45,000–$60,000

Despite the simplicity of its miter joints, this relatively flat, gilded frame designed by Stanford White consisted of row upon row of classic architectural elements. The design, consistent with the architect's training, was executed in 1907, after his death, by the Newcomb-Macklin Company and was widely copied thereafter. The crispness of ornamentation and the quality of surface gilding vary widely in those later simulations.

Courtesy of the Justine Simoni Collection

Price Ranges

14 × 20 inches:
$35,000–$40,000

24 × 36 inches:
$60,000–$95,000

36 × 48 inches:
$125,000–$200,000

This applied-compo gilded frame, designed by Stanford White in the 1890s, was given a unique surface decoration suggestive of snakeskin.

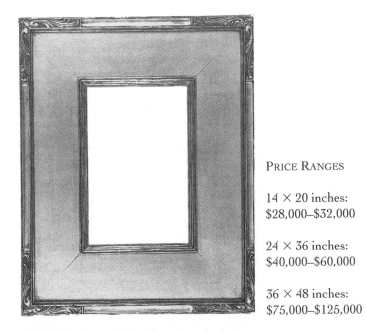

PRICE RANGES

14 × 20 inches:
$28,000–$32,000

24 × 36 inches:
$40,000–$60,000

36 × 48 inches:
$75,000–$125,000

Hermann Dudley Murphy designed and crafted this 1909 frame, which was carved and gilded, rather than molded. A style adapted from Venetian cassetta frames, it was the genesis of nearly all of the American impressionist-style frames that followed.

The mark of Murphy's firm, Carrig-Rohane, was incised on the back of the frame, along with the date of its completion.

Courtesy of the Justine Simoni Collection

PRICE RANGES

14 × 20 inches:
$55,000–$95,000

24 × 36 inches:
$150,000–$225,000

36 × 48 inches:
$225,000–$275,000

Carved, incised, and silvered, this frame is a rare, thus costly, example of a design crafted by Charles Prendergast. Combining incised floral designs with the creative use of silver gilding and shellac, the design was rendered soon after the turn of the twentieth century.

PRICE RANGES

14 × 20 inches:
$9,500–$16,000

24 × 36 inches:
$18,000–$24,000

36 × 48 inches:
$35,000–$45,000

A broad, flat, gilded frame with a tightly rendered floral design in applied compo typified much of the design seen in the 1890s.

Price Ranges

14 × 20 inches:
$20,000–$24,000

24 × 36 inches:
$28,000–$35,000

36 × 48 inches:
$40,000–$55,000

Despite its convex outer band, beading, and leaf and flower motifs, this gilded compo frame displays the restrained ornamentation and relatively flat profile that distinguish frame design of the period.

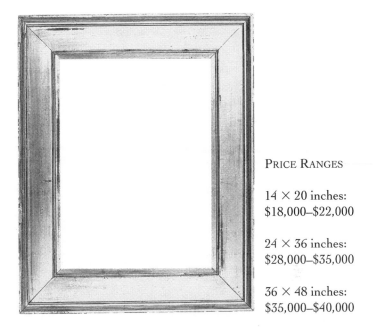

PRICE RANGES

14 × 20 inches:
$18,000–$22,000

24 × 36 inches:
$28,000–$35,000

36 × 48 inches:
$35,000–$40,000

The restrained use of ornamentation reached its apogee in the 1890s with spare, flat frames like this one, which were hand-carved and handsomely gilded. Less was, indeed, more in frames designed by major makers—this one carries the Doll & Richards label—to complement, rather than detract from, whatever paintings they enclosed.

PRICE RANGES

14 × 20 inches:
$22,000–$28,000

24 × 36 inches:
$30,000–$40,000

36 × 48 inches:
$45,000–$60,000

The circa-1890 version of a Whistler-style gilded compo frame affirms that the reeded moldings popularized by the expatriate artist James McNeill Whistler in the 1860s had at last found favor in the United States.

Tondo frame; carved, gilded and polychromed wood:
Michelangelo, "Madonna and Child," 1504.

Courtesy of Uffizi Gallery, Florence

18th-century American frame; carved and gilded wood:
"Mrs. Jerathmael Bowers" by John Singleton Copley, circa 1765.

Courtesy of the American Paintings Department,
Metropolitan Museum of Art, New York City

American frame (1880s); applied composition ornament and gilding, original to the painting by Henry Alexander. Approximate outside dimensions: 31½ inches x 35⅝ inches.

Courtesy of the Justine Simoni Collection

Detail of an early 20th-century American frame by Frederick Harer; carved, incised and gilded wood; framemaker's name "Harer" inscribed on back. Molding width: 3½ inches.

Courtesy of Eli Wilner & Company, Inc., New York City

Detail of an American Orientalist-style frame (1870s-1880s); applied composition ornament, incised decoration, wood and gilding. Molding width: 5 inches. Label on back of frame: "Noyes & Blakeslee, Boston, Massachusetts."

Courtesy of Eli Wilner & Company, Inc., New York City

Detail of 19th-century American frame (1830s); applied composition ornament, wood and gilding: "Study for Dream of Arcadia" by Thomas Cole, 1838. Approximate outside dimensions: 15¾ x 21½ inches.

Courtesy of the New York Historical Society, New York City

American frame (1850s); wood, applied composition ornament and gilding: "Shrewsbury River" by J. F. Kensett, 1859. Approximate outside dimensions: 30½ x 42½ inches.

Detail of above.

19th-century American frame; applied composition ornament, wood and gilding: "Morning at Grand Manan" by Alfred Bricher, 1878. Approximate outside dimensions: 40 x 65 inches.

Courtesy of the Indianapolis Museum of Art

Detail of above.

American frame (1890-1900); applied composition ornament, gilding applied directly to oak. Approximate outside dimensions: 24 x 30 inches.

Courtesy of Eli Wilner & Company, Inc., New York City

Early 20th-century American frame by Foster Brothers; carved and gilded wood, Foster Brothers label on verso. Approximate outside dimensions: 31½ inches x 35⅝ inches.

Courtesy of the Justine Simoni Collection

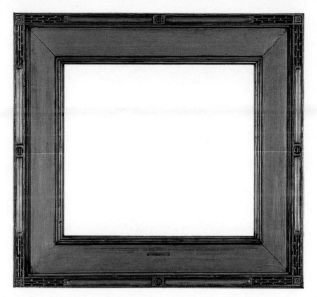

American frame designed by Childe Hassam, circa 1910; carved and gilded. (The artist's initials appear at midpoints.) Approximate outside dimensions: 31 x 34 inches.

Courtesy of the American Paintings Department,
Metropolitan Museum of Art, New York City

Detail of above.

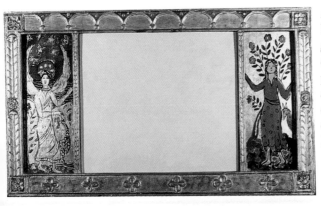

American mirror frame by Charles Prendergast, circa 1915-1918; carved wood with punchwork, incising and polychromed decoration. Approximate outside dimensions: 18 x 31 inches.

Courtesy of
Williams College
Museum of Art,
Williamstown,
Massachusetts

Early 20th-century American frame; carved and gilded wood: "Preparing for the Matinee" by Edmund Tarbell, 1907. Approximate outside dimensions: 42 x 52 inches.

Courtesy of the Indianapolis
Museum of Art

Detail of an American frame by Arthur and Lucia Mathews, circa 1910; carved, polychromed and gilded wood. Approximate outside dimensions: 35 x 39½ inches.

Early 20th-century American frame by Marsden Hartley; painted wood: "Flower Abstraction" by Marsden Hartley, 1914.

Private collection

20th-century American frame by John Marin; carved and painted wood: "Boat and Sea, Cape Split, Maine," by John Marin, 1938.

Private collection

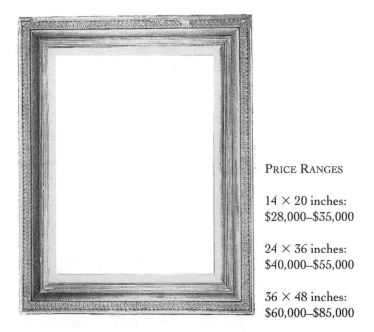

PRICE RANGES

14 × 20 inches:
$28,000–$35,000

24 × 36 inches:
$40,000–$55,000

36 × 48 inches:
$60,000–$85,000

The work of a highly regarded framemaker of the 1890s, this one is another relatively flat, restrained example in gilded compo. On the back is the artisan's label, "Dennis Dinan, New York."

PRICE RANGES

14 × 20 inches:
$18,000–$22,000

24 × 36 inches:
$25,000–$35,000

36 × 48 inches:
$40,000–$60,000

This gilded, applied-compo example reflects the shift in frame design taking place at the end of the nineteenth century. Combined with elaborate decorative elements along the outer edges is a series of flat panels that are rendered simply and unembellished.

PRICE RANGES

14 × 20 inches:
$12,000–$18,000

24 × 36 inches:
$22,000–$30,000

36 × 48 inches:
$30,000–$40,000

In this example of a popular style in the 1890s and early 1900s, the gesso layer was omitted in the frame-making process, and the gold leaf was applied directly to the wood, which was most often oak. This surface treatment, adopted by Whistler in some of his frame designs, produced a rich though subdued surface.

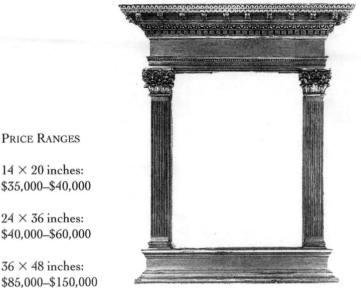

PRICE RANGES

14 × 20 inches:
$35,000–$40,000

24 × 36 inches:
$40,000–$60,000

36 × 48 inches:
$85,000–$150,000

This magnificent tabernacle frame of the 1890s illustrates the elegant detailing and richly layered gilding that typified the work of Foster Brothers, the Boston framemakers.

Courtesy of the Justine Simoni Collection

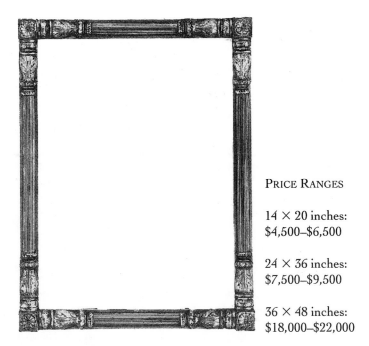

PRICE RANGES

14 × 20 inches:
$4,500–$6,500

24 × 36 inches:
$7,500–$9,500

36 × 48 inches:
$18,000–$22,000

Although crafted in the 1890s, this carved and gilded example with its linear ornamentation and restrained use of fluting confirms the ongoing legacy of American Renaissance design ideals born two decades earlier.

PART THREE

Early Twentieth-Century Frames

CHAPTER 10

1900-1919
Triumph of Handcraftsmanship

"THE most original and enchanting frames were crafted about the turn of the twentieth century by Charles Prendergast," writes George Szabo in his essay "Frames in America." Of Charles's frames, Szabo notes:

> They are in perfect harmony with his own paintings and with those of his brother, Maurice. . . . These frames not only enhance the pictures but sometimes assume a significance beyond their own so-called functional or secondary role—as works of art on their own merit.

Charles had begun making frames in about 1895 at Maurice's suggestion and with the encouragement of their talented neighbor Hermann Dudley Murphy. In 1903 Murphy built a new home and studio in Winchester, Massachusetts, which he named Carrig-Rohane, Gaelic for "red cliff," a salute to his father's Celtic heritage. The studio in the basement of his home became the site of his frame-making enterprise, which he established with Charles Prendergast as his first associate.

In 1905 the firm, also called Carrig-Rohane, moved to Boston. There, Murphy was to form an association with Walfred Thulin, a Swedish-born wood-carver who eventually opened his own frame shop on Boylston Street, not far from Carrig-Rohane. Thulin's distinctive monogram can be found on such diverse objects as trays, chests, and candlesticks as well as the elegant frames he created for John Singer Sargent, Frank W. Benson, and other leading Boston artists. His monogram sometimes took the form of the initial *T* set into a diamond shape; at other times, a *W* was superimposed on the *T* within that diamond. But often his last name was simply incised on the back of a frame.

Meanwhile, Murphy's work helped establish Boston as the center of frame design in America; his characteristic flat, unadorned frames were seen as the perfect complements to the impressionist paintings gaining favor at the time. In her essay in *Antiques & Fine Art* magazine, Suzanne Smeaton writes:

> The flat profile would show to best advantage the subtleties of the gilding process acknowledged years earlier by Whistler. Many new shades of gilding were used on the frames to best harmonize with the canvases they surrounded.

As Whistler was also a Celt, he and Murphy were linked by more than talent, profession, and a shared belief in the total perception of a work of art. Smeaton points out that Whistler and Murphy also had in common "their habit of signing their frames. But Murphy's influence on American framemaking was far greater than Whistler's." The name of Murphy's firm was incised on the back of his frames, whereas Whistler's signature was actually a butterfly monogram that appeared discreetly on the face of his frames.

Before turning over his Carrig-Rohane shares to the artisans he employed, Murphy was crafting frames not only for his own work but also for such discriminating artists as Childe Hassam, William Merritt Chase, and Emil Carlsen. In 1917 the firm was sold to the Vose Galleries of Boston, Inc., which kept it in business through the 1940s.

Frame design in the early twentieth century was shaped by an overriding need to be sympathetic to the colors and brushwork of a whole new generation of artists. The shift away from complex frame profiles dense with applied ornament was also a reaction to and rejection of the mass production that had come to dominate late-nineteenth-century industry in America.

Until about 1915 the simple, sensuous elegance of art nouveau enjoyed a rush of popularity. Taking inspiration from Gothic revival

and rococo revival elements, and from Japanese graphic art, American art nouveau frames were readily identifiable by their ornament, which included plant, flower, leaf, and tendril motifs. In addition, writes Virginia V. Van Rees:

> Art nouveau frame designers would take asymmetry and curvilinear shapes and extend them to include both ornament and form. This was a period of light (as opposed to heavy) design, and it is reflected in its frames.

The early twentieth century was also a time when framemakers gave their works the imprimatur of fine art. Murphy, for one, made certain the name of his firm appeared on the back of each frame he fashioned, along with the date of its completion. After Carrig-Rohane was sold, the name continued to appear right above that of

Vose. Foster Brothers of Boston affixed brass medallions to the backs of their frames, each one identifying the firm as "Makers."

Charles Prendergast continued to flourish as a framemaker long after ending his Murphy partnership, with "Prendergast" proudly incised onto the back of his work. Indeed, framemaking provided a greater career impetus for him and his brother than the work of either man as an artist. Their move from Winchester, Massachusetts, to Boston was made possible by a single frame, commissioned by a Boston financier. Nine years later, their 1914 move from Boston to New York was funded by an order for frames to set off the portraits of eighteen past presidents of a Philadelphia insurance company.

The brothers must have been fairly well established members of the New York art world for some time before that last move, however, for it is known that Charles supplied a number of frames for the landmark Armory Show of 1913. During the course of his career, he created some four hundred pieces, among them a group commissioned to enclose paintings in the famous Barnes Collection in Merion, Pennsylvania.

Boston may have been the locus of American framemaking in the first two decades of the twentieth century, but it was not the only supplier. Nor did every popular frame style necessarily have a European antecedent. The Newcomb-Macklin Company, with offices in New York and Chicago, established links with artists as far afield as Taos, New Mexico, and in ornamenting much of its work, drew inspiration from Native American design traditions. Thus their frames surround the paintings of such important southwestern artists as Walter Ufer and E. Martin Hennings, in addition to eastern painters including Maxfield Parrish, George Bellows, and, once again, John Singer Sargent.

The Newcomb-Macklin Company appears to have been most productive during the early years of the century, maintaining an extensive stock of ready-made frames—in standard sizes and a variety of finishes—along with a comprehensive selection of styles for custom work. The firm also executed Stanford White frame designs after the architect's death in 1906.

At about this time, Bucks County, Pennsylvania, was becoming another notable frame center, largely because of Frederick Harer, a well-traveled painter, sculptor, etcher, and framemaker who lived and worked in the town of New Hope. The son of a successful furnituremaker, Harer learned woodworking as a youth and later used his father's tools to execute many of his frame designs, which utilized stenciling, incising, matte and burnished gilding, and punchwork—patterns hammered into a frame surface with nails he had cut and filed down for that purpose.

Harer's frames, which reflect Spanish and West Indian influences absorbed from his travels, adorned his own work plus that of other Bucks County artists, including Daniel Garber and Edward Redfield. He said he believed that all his designs were "based on fundamental truths that I hope will survive this period and all others, as the primitives have done." Writes Suzanne Smeaton, "Indeed, his design motifs—a unique blend of naïveté and sophistication—stand today as a powerful testament to his vision."

Bernard "Ben" Badura, one of Harer's students and devoted friends, created frames that were a synthesis of his mentor's aesthetics combined with the modernist views of Arthur B. Carles, under whom he studied at the Pennsylvania Academy of Fine Art. Another New Hope artisan, Francis Coll, was recognized as much for his frames as for his paintings and craftsmanship of ecclesiastical subjects. And Cullen Yates, who hailed from Monroe County, Pennsylvania, was a recognized landscape painter who came under the early influence of William Merritt Chase, a well-known frame enthusiast. Writes Suzanne Smeaton, in her summation:

> Almost all of these innovators paid special attention to the subtleties of the gilding process. Many experimented with the many possible tonalities of gold and also with white gold and silver leaf.

Although quality framemaking had a greater presence in the eastern part of the United States, the California artists Arthur and Lucia Mathews were making a substantive contribution at the same time. Arthur brought his early training as an architect to his work as an artist and to creating his frames, whose designs were shaped by the influence of Whistler. Arthur's wife, Lucia Kleinhans, a talented artist in her own right, met him at the California School of Design in San Francisco in 1893, and worked with him thereafter. Their frames embodied a variety of woods, painted surfaces, and inlay, plus a unique method of flat-relief carving the Mathewses taught their craftsmen.

Through the Furniture Shop, which they established after the 1906 San Francisco earthquake and fire, they marketed two types of picture frames. The first consisted of simple but original moldings painted to complement the tones of the paintings they framed. The second type was more elaborate and thematic, incorporating architectural elements, Oriental designs, and natural motifs associated with California: cypress trees, oranges, and the state flower, the poppy. When World War I created a scarcity of both craftsmen and materials on the west coast, the Furniture Shop struggled to stay in business and finally shut its doors in 1920.

By the early twentieth century, framemaking had made a six-hundred-year odyssey from artisan's shop to cabinetmaker's workroom to artist's studio, changing its profile but never deviating from its purpose. "The frame presents rather than imprisons the work of art," wrote Richard B. Brettell in an essay introducing the catalog for the 1986 frame retrospective at The Art Institute of Chicago.

Taking that idea a step further, Joy De Weese-Wehen, in a 1990 issue of *Antique Monthly*, insisted, "To the art purist the ideal frame is the one you don't notice," although acknowledging that there have been times when frames "began to rival—and sometimes even surpass—the paintings they were only supposed to complement." Her conclusion:

> Without the visual brakes of a well-defined border, the eye wanders quickly away from the more demanding complexity of a picture to the comfortable blankness of the surrounding wall. The result can be an oddly queasy disorientation. The earliest artists did not know the psychological reason—they were only aware that when they put a frame around their picture, it looked better.

PRICE LISTINGS

Price Ranges

14 × 20 inches:
$55,000–$95,000

24 × 36 inches:
$150,000–$225,000

36 × 48 inches:
$225,000–$275,000

Charles Prendergast designed and crafted this circa-1905 frame, which had incised and punchwork decoration.

Courtesy of the Justine Simoni Collection

PRICE RANGES

14 × 20 inches:
$35,000–$65,000

24 × 36 inches:
$75,000–$125,000

36 × 48 inches:
$140,000–$165,000

Designed and crafted by Charles Prendergast in about 1905, and with "Prendergast" incised on the back, this gilded frame is distinguished by its French provincial inspiration and by surface decoration that was hand-carved, not molded.

Courtesy of the Justine Simoni Collection

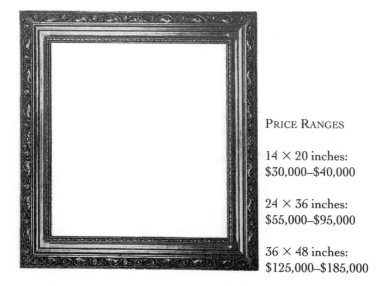

PRICE RANGES

14 × 20 inches:
$30,000–$40,000

24 × 36 inches:
$55,000–$95,000

36 × 48 inches:
$125,000–$185,000

This hand-carved, gilded frame is the work of Hermann Dudley Murphy, whose firm's name, Carrig-Rohane, and the year the frame was crafted, 1909, were incised on the back. The openwork carving shows Murphy's skillful hand.

PRICE RANGES

14 × 20 inches:
$30,000–$40,000

24 × 36 inches:
$55,000–$95,000

36 × 48 inches:
$125,000–$185,000

This hand-carved frame with its incised and punched-surface decoration was designed and crafted by Hermann Dudley Murphy. His firm's name, Carrig-Rohane, was
incised on the back along with the year of the frame's execution, 1905.

Private collection

Price Ranges

14 × 20 inches:
$30,000–$40,000

24 × 36 inches:
$55,000–$95,000

36 × 48 inches:
$125,000–$185,000

Signed and dated "Carrig-Rohane 1909," this hand-carved, gilded frame was designed and crafted by Hermann Dudley Murphy.

PRICE RANGES

14 × 20 inches:
$30,000–$35,000

24 × 36 inches:
$45,000–$85,000

36 × 48 inches:
$95,000–$150,000

Walfred Thulin designed and crafted this gilded frame, which bears the year it was carved and gilded, 1922, and the artist's name on the back.

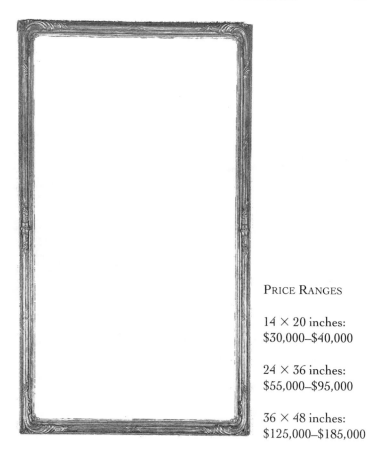

Price Ranges

14 × 20 inches:
$30,000–$40,000

24 × 36 inches:
$55,000–$95,000

36 × 48 inches:
$125,000–$185,000

Curved hand-carved decorative motifs in the corners, cross-straps, and discreet ornamentation on the center panels are all that interrupt the linear elegance of this gilded frame designed and crafted by Walfred Thulin. It is incribed "THULIN 1923" on the back.

Courtesy of the Justine Simoni Collection

PRICE RANGES

14 × 20 inches:
$30,000–$40,000

24 × 36 inches:
$45,000–$85,000

36 × 48 inches:
$95,000–$150,000

Childe Hassam designed this gilded frame in 1920, including his initial H as a principal motif. The frame was crafted by the Royal Art Company in New York City.

Courtesy of the Justine Simoni Collection

PRICE RANGES

14 × 20 inches:
$30,000–$40,000

24 × 36 inches:
$55,000–$85,000

36 × 48 inches:
$125,000–$185,000

This circa-1910 frame, crafted by Foster Brothers, reflects the influence of seventeenth-century Dutch design. The corners, with right-angle extensions that widen the profile at those points, are reinterpretations of the crossetted corners often found on Dutch frames.

PRICE RANGES

14 × 20 inches:
$30,000–$40,000

24 × 36 inches:
$55,000–$85,000

36 × 48 inches:
$125,000–$185,000

Made in 1910 by Foster Brothers, the Boston framemaker, this gilded frame has incised leaf and flower motifs at the center of each panel and hand-carved leaves that extend around the corners.

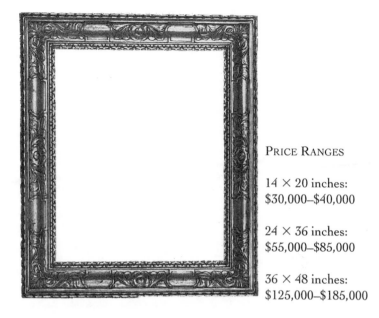

PRICE RANGES

14 × 20 inches:
$30,000–$40,000

24 × 36 inches:
$55,000–$85,000

36 × 48 inches:
$125,000–$185,000

Hand-carved floral motifs plus incised patterning enrich this gilded frame, circa 1910. A Foster Brothers medallion on the back affirms its origin.

PRICE RANGES

14 × 20 inches:
$28,000–$35,000

24 × 36 inches:
$45,000–$85,000

36 × 48 inches:
$150,000–$200,000

Here's a fine example of custom frame design by the Newcomb-Macklin Company during the early years of the twentieth century. It was hand-carved and gilded, around 1910.

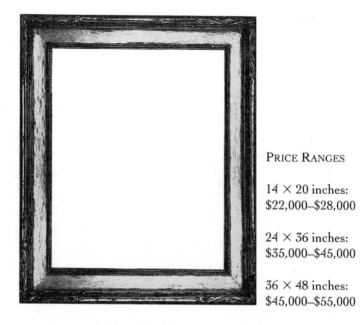

PRICE RANGES

14 × 20 inches:
$22,000–$28,000

24 × 36 inches:
$35,000–$45,000

36 × 48 inches:
$45,000–$55,000

A flat, unornamented surface dominates this circa-1910 frame, carved and gilded by the Newcomb-Macklin Company. Its style was one that was widely popular in the early years of the century.

PRICE RANGES

14 × 20 inches:
$28,000–$35,000

24 × 36 inches:
$38,000–$55,000

36 × 48 inches:
$65,000–$125,000

Crafted in America in 1903, this frame is truest to a design made by James McNeill Whistler back in the 1860s. It is multibanded, carved, and gilded, with the reeded molding that became popular in the United States early in the twentieth century.

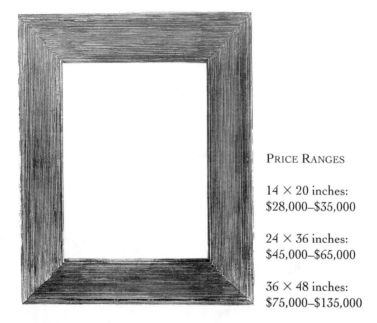

Price Ranges

14 × 20 inches:
$28,000–$35,000

24 × 36 inches:
$45,000–$65,000

36 × 48 inches:
$75,000–$135,000

Here is another variation, circa 1900, of a hand-carved, gilded frame in the Whistler style. Nearly all frames that employed the generous use of reeded elements were considered Whistler style, as many different combinations were possible.

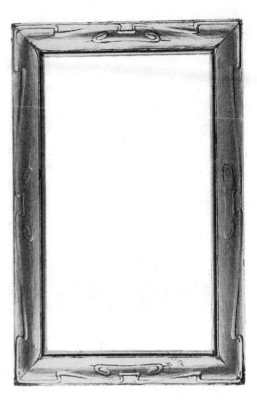

PRICE RANGES

14 × 20 inches:
$28,000–$35,000

24 × 36 inches:
$40,000–$55,000

36 × 48 inches:
$65,000–$85,000

The soft, subtle influence of art nouveau and Native American design shape the hand-carved decoration on this circa-1910 gilded frame fashioned by Frederick Loeser of Brooklyn, New York. His label appears on the back.

Courtesy of the Justine Simoni Collection

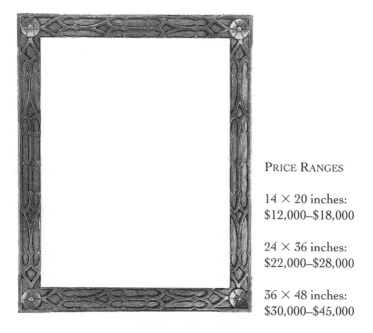

PRICE RANGES

14 × 20 inches:
$12,000–$18,000

24 × 36 inches:
$22,000–$28,000

36 × 48 inches:
$30,000–$45,000

Gothic style experienced an unexpected renaissance in the early 1900s, as shown in this carved, gilded frame crafted about 1910.

Courtesy of the Justine Simoni Collection

PRICE RANGES

14 × 20 inches:
$12,000–$18,000

24 × 36 inches:
$22,000–$28,000

36 × 48 inches:
$30,000–$40,000

Hand-carved elegance from graceful, curving designs proliferated in the early years of the twentieth century. The unsigned gilded frame in this detail was made about 1910.

PRICE RANGES

14 × 20 inches:
$22,000–$32,000

24 × 36 inches:
$35,000–$45,000

36 × 48 inches:
$55,000–$75,000

Hand-carved, gilded frames like this one represent the Taos style, so named because it was typical of frames found on paintings of the American Southwest and its design draws upon Native American decorative elements.

PRICE RANGES

14 × 20 inches:
$30,000–$40,000

24 × 36 inches:
$50,000–$85,000

36 × 48 inches:
$125,000–$185,000

This hand-carved frame, with an incised zigzag pattern on each of its major elements, was designed and crafted circa 1910 by Frederick Harer. Gilded in silver rather than gold leaf, the frame bears Harer's signature on the back.

Price Ranges

14 × 20 inches:
$30,000–$40,000

24 × 36 inches:
$50,000–$85,000

36 × 48 inches:
$125,000–$185,000

Authenticated by the signature on the back, this hand-carved gilded frame with its strong Italian influence was designed and crafted by Frederick Harer around 1910.

PRICE RANGES

14 × 20 inches:
$30,000–$40,000

24 × 36 inches:
$50,000–$85,000

36 × 48 inches:
$125,000–$185,000

Punchwork corner decoration and incised motifs distinguish this hand-carved gilded frame designed and crafted by Frederick Harer, circa 1910. His signature appears on the back.

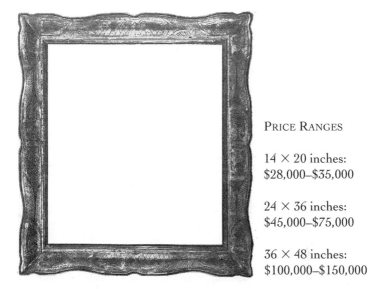

PRICE RANGES

14 × 20 inches:
$28,000–$35,000

24 × 36 inches:
$45,000–$75,000

36 × 48 inches:
$100,000–$150,000

Bernard "Ben" Badura, a student of Harer's, gave a unique shape to this frame, which he designed and crafted around 1920. It is hand-carved, incised, and silver-gilded, with his signature inscribed on the back.

PRICE RANGES

14 × 20 inches:
$22,000–$28,000

24 × 36 inches:
$30,000–$40,000

36 × 48 inches:
$45,000–$65,000

Here is an example of Francis Coll's work, which carries his signature, a frame that was hand-carved and incised, then silver-gilded, circa 1920.

Courtesy of the Justine Simoni Collection

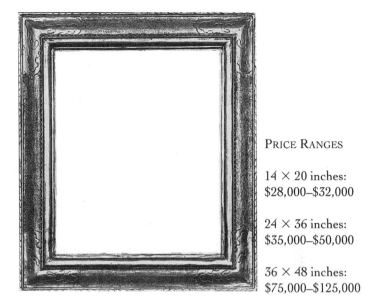

PRICE RANGES

14 × 20 inches:
$28,000–$32,000

24 × 36 inches:
$35,000–$50,000

36 × 48 inches:
$75,000–$125,000

This carved, incised, gilded frame, designed and crafted around 1920, was signed by the artist and craftsman Cullen Yates.

PRICE RANGES

14 × 20 inches:
$55,000–$75,000

24 × 36 inches:
$85,000–$125,000

36 × 48 inches:
$150,000–$185,000

Not gilded, this circa-1910 hand-carved tabernacle frame, designed and crafted by Californians Arthur and Lucia Mathews, was stained olive green instead.

Courtesy of the Oakland Museum

PRICE RANGES

14 × 20 inches:
$65,000–$100,000

24 × 36 inches:
$125,000–$175,000

36 × 48 inches:
$180,000–$250,000

Another tabernacle frame designed and crafted by Arthur and Lucia Mathews, this hand-carved example was both stained and gilded.

Courtesy of the Oakland Museum

PRICE RANGES

14 × 20 inches:
$28,000–$35,000

24 × 36 inches:
$40,000–$65,000

36 × 48 inches:
$85,000–$150,000

Max Kuehne, a friend and protégé of Charles Prendergast, designed and crafted this circa-1915 frame, which, like many of his pieces, was similar to his mentor's work in its use of a cassetta profile, incised decoration, and silver gilding.

Courtesy of the Justine Simoni Collection

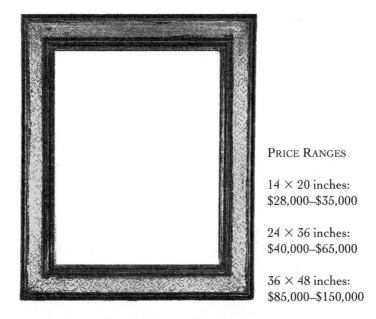

PRICE RANGES

14 × 20 inches:
$28,000–$35,000

24 × 36 inches:
$40,000–$65,000

36 × 48 inches:
$85,000–$150,000

Here is another Max Kuehne frame, circa 1915, which was hand-carved and silver-gilded before being incised with decoration.

PRICE RANGES

14 × 20 inches:
$35,000–$45,000

24 × 36 inches:
$85,000–$150,000

36 × 48 inches:
$165,000–$185,000

This is a uniquely elegant circa-1910 frame with sophisticated carving and a richly gilded surface. A label on the back attributes the frame to the work of the J. H. Miller Company of Springfield, Massachusetts.

Courtesy of the Justine Simoni Collection

CHAPTER 11

1920-1939
The Integration Urge

It wasn't only the Furniture Shop, established by Arthur and Lucia Mathews in San Francisco, that was affected by the onset of World War I and the disappearance of trained craftsmen from the civilian workplace into the military. Gold was in short supply, too, as were the gilders who customarily worked with it. Almost overnight, the American tradition of framemaking that had begun rather shakily with the arrival of the first colonists, centuries earlier, was thrust into disarray. By the time the Armistice was signed, new alternatives to traditional frame-making techniques had begun to achieve prominence.

Although wood remained the framing material of choice, coatings other than gold came into wide use in the 1920s: aluminum gilding, silver, chrome, and painted surfaces. "The interesting evolution and material culture of American picture frames chronicles the evolution of decorative and artistic trends in America," writes Virginia V. Van Rees. So it was predictable that the art deco style would influence framemaking as it swept across the decorative arts spectrum during the years between the two world wars.

Streamlining was in vogue, with wing and airplane motifs appearing prominently in everything from textile patterns to automobile design. Circles, zigzags, and other geometric patterns were also recognizable earmarks of art deco, a term derived from the first comprehensive decorative arts exhibition, held in Paris in 1925. The genesis of art deco is traceable to the purity and simplicity of the International Style, whose principal proponent, Le Corbusier, had been one of the founders of the Bauhaus School.

Art deco was a movement entirely separate unto itself; not every artist or craftsman at work in those interim decades embraced it or furthered it in any way. So in terms of frame design, this cannot be identified as the art deco period. If there is any term that, for me, fully describes what was taking place in the world of frame design in the 1920s and 1930s, it would be "free-form." The creativity of the artists themselves, rather than any new or long-established tradition, was what determined the several directions frame design would take. "The Arts and Crafts idea of the totality of art and environment was expanded upon," writes Suzanne Smeaton, for this was a time when art and frame became virtually inseparable and mutually dependent. She cites Marsden Hartley, whose "frames of the teens . . . go beyond contemplating the artwork; they are integral to the composition." Other artists of equal prominence nationally—among them John Marin, Arthur Dove, Charles Demuth, Edward Hopper, and Charles Sheeler—were deeply committed to frame design. Their singular efforts signaled the end of the traditional approach to framemaking in America.

Marin had a colorful way with frame design, often painting his flat wood borders in brushstrokes and colors that complemented his art. He also had a penchant for extending his painted imagery beyond the paper or canvas and onto the flat surface of the wooden frame that surrounded it. Thus, in so many instances, frame and picture became one. According to Smeaton's description:

> Often frames made by the artists of this period have a specific home-crafted quality; indeed, many of these frames seen by themselves can appear to be crudely constructed and naive in their design. When seen together with the artworks they were made for, the sensitivity and pertinence of their design becomes apparent.

If there is no single theme apparent in the evolution of frame design in the 1920s and 1930s, blame can be laid in large part on the troubled state of the art world at that time. Social unrest and the rise of various political movements developed inroads of influence, frequently shaping artistic expression. Ostensibly this was the time when modernism was in full flower, but I have never considered it so much a movement as an approach to making art. "Between the two wars, the only major international art movements to arise were dada and its offspring, surrealism," writes art critic Barbara Rose in her seminal book *American Art Since 1900*. It was a time when the avant-garde was struggling to find its voice and when the celebrated German artist-émigré Hans Hofmann was transplanting his European-based ideas of "forming with color" to American students at the school he founded in New York.

Two young painters who would one day be lionized in the pantheon of European-born American artists—Jackson Pollock and Willem de Kooning—would begin grappling with their own compelling artistic visions during the decade just after World War I. According to Rose, "Each in his own manner struggled with the genius of Picasso, and in his struggle, helped free American art permanently from its European ancestry."

Of all the artists who were passionately committed to frame design, it was John Marin who best defined the free-form spirit of the times in work that demonstrated the interdependency of frame design and art. "If I were younger," he once told an interviewer, "I'd plunge into sculpture, but my framemaking will have to satisfy my sculptural urges." According to Ruth E. Fine, in her definitive work *John Marin*:

> As the years passed, Marin's frames became increasingly complex. The later paintings became ever more explosive, more calligraphic, with the artist more attentive to an overall quality of surface as well as to the development of spatial activity. . . . Marin constructed, carved, and painted his frames. . . . In this way, he modified the edges of his images by extending them yet another level, into the world of the viewer.

Marin's frames were commercially made and then modified, usually with paint, but he was also known to fashion frames himself—from cut wood or from driftwood and other found materials. By the 1930s Marin's frames had become such an accepted extension of his art that they received comment along with the oil paintings and watercolors they enclosed. In 1937 a New York art critic, Ralph Flint, described one of Marin's found-wood examples as "a frame that will have its place in present-day Americana as sure as collectors are collectors." But perhaps the most eloquent testimonial to John Marin's frame design and to the integration of art and frame that characterized this era was delivered by another critic, Herbert Seligmann, in published notes for a gallery show opening in late 1933:

> And so, when at last he came to present these pictures, it was inevitable and a happy movement of genius that he should play in the frames in the same spirit of invention, daring, and fertility that he had played with the forces of nature speaking through him in the watercolors and oils.

As far as I am concerned, no era could have a finer or more appropriate epitaph.

PRICE LISTINGS

PRICE RANGES

14 × 20 inches:
$12,000–$18,000

24 × 36 inches:
$22,000–$32,000

36 × 48 inches:
$35,000–$45,000

The art deco influence brought angular understatement to frame design, as seen in this hand-carved, silver-gilded example circa 1920.

PRICE RANGES

14 × 20 inches:
$12,000–$16,000

24 × 36 inches:
$18,000–$24,000

36 × 48 inches:
$28,000–$35,000

Although generally flat rather than angular, this carved, silver-gilded frame presents another example of art deco inspiration, circa 1920.

PRICE RANGES

14 × 20 inches:
$18,000–$22,000

24 × 36 inches:
$24,000–$35,000

36 × 48 inches:
$38,000–$45,000

Carved, painted, and rubbed—that is, hand-distressed—this frame is similar to those found on the paintings of Marsden Hartley in the 1920s and 1930s. The boldly carved forms echo Hartley's own brushstrokes.

PRICE RANGES

14 × 20 inches:
$16,000–$20,000

24 × 36 inches:
$22,000–$28,000

36 × 48 inches:
$30,000–$38,000

Carved in wood, this frame would have been rubbed with paint rather than gilded. Dating from the 1920s or 1930s, or possibly later, it typifies the frames with simplified forms and strong surface textures that so often enclosed modernist paintings.

PRICE RANGES

14 × 20 inches:
$16,000–$20,000

24 × 36 inches:
$22,000–$28,000

36 × 48 inches:
$30,000–$38,000

The coarse, uneven wood surface of this frame, typical of the 1920s and 1930s, is combined with carved designs that are both graceful and sophisticated.

PRICE RANGES

14 × 20 inches:
$16,000–$20,000

24 × 36 inches:
$22,000–$28,000

36 × 48 inches:
$30,000–$38,000

Carved, painted, and rubbed, the wood surface of this frame is an example of that found on frames crafted by artists during the years between the wars. Though not strikingly beautiful on their own, these frames were nonetheless integral to the paintings they surrounded and to their presentation. Often the colors and uneven textures were extensions of the work within.

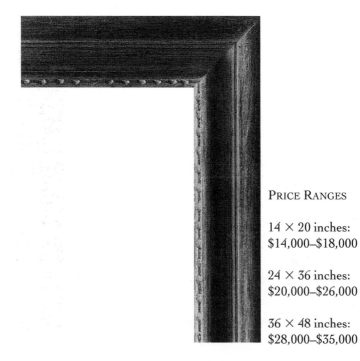

PRICE RANGES

14 × 20 inches:
$14,000–$18,000

24 × 36 inches:
$20,000–$26,000

36 × 48 inches:
$28,000–$35,000

Very likely machine-carved and then stained, this is the type of frame that would have been selected by artists seeking to frame their work in the most economical way. Simply rendered and largely undecorated, it blended well with the modernist painting style of the 1930s.

PRICE RANGES

14 × 20 inches:
$14,000–$18,000

24 × 36 inches:
$20,000–$26,000

36 × 48 inches:
$28,000–$35,000

In this detail of a modernist-style frame from the 1930s, you can see the hand-distressed surface that was created after the molding itself was carved and painted. Angles, curves, and dentil-style ornament give the frame distinction.

PART FOUR

Trade Secrets

CHAPTER 12

Cleaning, Handling, and Documenting Period Frames

Nineteenth- and early-twentieth-century picture frames were done primarily in high relief with elaborate patterns. They borrowed themes, moods, and styles from various epochs in art, architecture, and furniture design. A frame bearing the signature of the artist or framemaker who crafted it is obviously more significant than one with no identification marks at all. Signed frames from the early twentieth century are rare nowadays, but many do turn up occasionally. Signatures can usually be found on the back of a frame. Most of the time, framemakers marked their work with a paper label, a fragile form of identification that usually peeled off or was simply lost with the passing years.

An antique frame with a name or label on the back can be extremely valuable, but a frame need not be signed and numbered to command a substantial price. The quality of the workmanship and the condition of the gilding are important price factors. So is authenticity.

A knowledgeable dealer or collector will know almost immediately whether an item is the real thing or a fabrication. This is as true for antique picture frames as for paintings and sculpture. To confirm the authenticity of an old frame, you must not only have a sure eye but also a sure hand. Touching an item will often tell you as much as you can learn from looking at it, and the front of a frame is only half of the story. To make a proper and complete assessment, you will have to turn the frame around and examine the back.

Perhaps the best approach to educating yourself is to try and understand what an antique frame *isn't*. Once you recognize a frame to be a reproduction, for example, you may have to probe no further or be concerned about its style or age. Only authenticity will give a frame undeniable value.

Checking for Quality

You can assume a frame is a reproduction or has been regilded if:

- *splatter marks are visible on it, especially around the edges.* Reproduction gold-leaf frames frequently have a wash over them to diffuse the brightness of the gold and imitate the patina of age. The finish on reproduction frames often appears brassy and slick.
- *the patterns on the frame are soft and ill defined.* Authentic old frames will have crisp, clear patterns, whether carved in wood or molded. The possibility exists, of course, that an old frame has a completely new surface.
- *the wood on the back of the frame does not feel or look old.* A true antique will show recognizable signs of age—overall darkening, a surface roughened by handling—and the wood will *not* appear to have a new kind of finish on it. Old, rusted nails or other residual hardware will also confirm that the frame is old.
- *the frame is a combination of elements but was obviously milled from one piece of wood.* Turn the frame around so you can examine the back. An antique frame made up of a combination of patterns—it may look like a frame within a frame, for example—is likely to have been crafted from two or more pieces of molding joined together.

In trying to assess the quality of a frame, look carefully at the detail work; you can do this without turning the frame around or even lifting it off the wall. Up close, the patterns should be sharply rendered like pieces of fine jewelry. Each leaf, each flower, and every element in the design should be elegantly sculpted, with an enormous amount of fine detailing. Generally, the finer the detail work, the more valuable the frame.

If, instead of having been gold-leafed, a frame has been painted gold, it is undoubtedly new or was recently reworked. One relatively simple and fairly discreet way to make the distinction is with this test, which you can perform with your own finger: Touch the frame with the tip of your nail. If the surface really *is* gold, some parts of it are likely to be reflective; you will see a recognizable mirror image of your fingernail in that portion of the frame that was burnished. The deeper and brighter the reflection, the more gold there is. What you hope to see is a highly burnished surface. If paint has been used rather than gold leaf, however, the surface will appear dull and you will see no reflection. Water gilding produces a bright finish; oil gilding does not. But even an oil-gilded surface will have a depth of sheen that a painted surface lacks.

Another similar test can be made with anything you happen to be carrying that is made of gold: a watch, a chain, a ring, or an earring. Hold that object right beside the frame and see if a similarity exists. If, indeed, the frame is gold, it will have a close affinity to the depth and beauty of the test object. If the surface is gold paint, there will be no discernible depth — no real brightness and, once again, no reflection. The difference may be subtle, but if you look closely, you will see it.

Painting versus Gilding

The so-called quick fix has been a twentieth-century response to a great many problems, but in so many instances the quick fix is only a temporary and not very satisfying solution. It tends to create new problems or compound those that already exist. This is certainly true of antique picture frames.

Historically, the person who owned or bought an old frame with a damaged surface was not always eager to invest money in making professional-quality repairs or take the time and trouble to find a qualified restorer to do the job. Many of these unwitting and possibly unwilling collectors may have tried to make the repairs themselves. If gold leaf wasn't readily available or they didn't know how to work with it, they would settle for radiator paint, which was inexpensive and could be brushed or sprayed on. Instead of trying to restore the chipped, cracked, or crumbling sections of a frame, they would simply paint the whole unit a bright gold, coating the problems rather than solving them. Also, many did not understand the distinct difference between actual gold leaf and gold paint. When gold paint has been removed from a frame treated this way, the original gold-leaf surface may shine through. But the process of removing paint should be left to an experienced frame restorer, an established painting conservator, or a qualified furniture restorer.

Precursor to Restoration

How do you know if a restorer is qualified? Look carefully at some of his or her work—trust your eye. And listen to what you are being told. If the restorer advises you to strip the frame, removing all the gold, forget it. Turn around and walk out! This is not the person to put your trust in or entrust your picture frame to.

Back in the early 1980s I clipped a *New York Times* article that advocated getting all that ugly gold stuff off of old frames and exposing all that wonderful wood. *Ridiculous.* First of all, a gilded carved-wood frame is so valuable, it is absolutely inconceivable that anyone would want to strip it. Second, a molded frame reduced to its plasterlike composition material would be unattractive—and fundamentally worthless. Dipping old frames into an acid bath, or even into water, would almost certainly destroy the important frame legacy we are trying to protect and sustain. A stripped frame, no matter how old or how handsomely detailed, has little historical or monetary value.

Let's say, however, that you are attracted to a vintage frame at a flea market. It's painted; you're sure of that. But you don't know if there is any gilding beneath the coats of paint. Before you complete the purchase or make a bid, ask the seller if you can *test* the finish—with your saliva. If the answer is yes, lick the tip of a cotton swab and touch it to one corner of the frame. There is an enzyme in saliva that will cut through the coating of dirt where the saliva touches it and reveal the gold, if any, under it. Or use a cotton swab or a corner of your handkerchief to dab on a tiny amount of acetone, which will safely cut through any paint or darkened lacquer.

If acetone or your saliva removed some paint as well as grime, you can rest assured that, though the frame itself may be old, the paint was applied recently — because it is obviously water-based. That is why your saliva can dissolve and remove it. Any paint applied early in the twentieth century most likely would have been oil-based, and removal is tricky, thus not recommended. My advice would be to bypass a frame that is painted until you can determine what lies just beneath the surface — or be content to appreciate it as is. And whenever you set off on a quest for frames, be sure to bring along a vial of acetone as well as some cotton swabs. Always ask permission before testing the finish of any frame you fancy.

Also, be sure to test the frame surface in five or six spots — tiny quarter-inch tests, to be sure. You may well find that only one square inch of the frame is gold — probably in the corners — and the rest was coated originally in gold varnish, another cheap way of achieving coverage. As you remove the paint, the varnish will come off too — there is no way to save it. So you might end up with a frame stripped bare except for four gold corners, which is not desirable at all. Thus unless you can test the frame finish in several different spots, to see if paint comes off and gold leaf lies underneath, it is inadvisable to invest much money in such a frame. Even if you like it a lot, you would be taking a risk.

If applications of saliva or acetone fail to yield revealing results, you are probably better off not owning the frame, unless the price is right and you particularly like the look of it. Consider such a frame only a decorating element, not an investment. Whatever you do, *don't* spend money on stripping and regilding; find another, worthier example instead — it's better to err on the side of caution — unless, of course, you somehow happen on a Thomas Cole–designed frame surrounding one of his own signed works. Then, of course, you would want to put money into that frame's restoration.

It is possible to find a frame that hasn't been gilded but at some point was supposed to be. Gilding such an example, like regilding a stripped frame, is not recommended unless performed by master craftsmen. The process may well improve the object's appearance but will definitely reduce its potential value. The cost of regilding a frame properly can be justified only if a frame is a particularly rare example or has historic or sentimental value.

When you remove paint, don't be surprised if you discover silver underneath. American framemakers of the mid-nineteenth century often used silver leaf, then put ocher shellac over it, rendering the look of gold. So if you take the paint off or succeed in removing the ocher shellac, you will end up with silver—which, as a matter of fact, could be interesting.

Overall, I think it sad that so many fine, old frames have been destroyed, and so many more have been threatened, by being stripped to bare wood. To make an extreme comparison, it would be like taking an original Monet and removing all the paint just to reveal the texture of the canvas.

Cleaning an Old Frame

Once you get a frame home from the flea market or down from the attic where it has been gathering dust, you will undoubtedly want to clean it thoroughly, for only then will you know what you really have. Before touching your frame other than to dust it, consult someone at your local museum who is knowledgeable about frames. If yours is rare or especially valuable, you should not attempt to clean it yourself. If your consultant says it's all right to proceed, be sure to clean your frame with a soft camel's-hair brush; the brush attachment on your vacuum cleaner will be useful in collecting the dust. Frame conservators at the Metropolitan Museum of Art generally use cotton swabs and saliva in preparing their frames for a major exhibit.

Even if your old frame is nearly black with grime, do not simply attack its surface with detergent. Work slowly and carefully, cleaning one small section at a time. As with any work of art, handle with care—and always work on a padded surface to prevent damage. A sheet of plastic bubble wrap used for packing fragile goods makes an ideal cushion.

Be gentle, too, as you work. To test the effectiveness of your technique, try cleaning one spot on the side of your frame—a spot not highly visible—and then step back. See how much of the patina has come off. It is quite easy, as you become immersed in the cleaning process, to go too deep too fast. The dirt comes off and then the paint, until the gold is seen. Terrific—except there is a danger that the microscopically thin layer of lacquer, plus its accompanying patination, might come off too. What remains, after that layer has been removed, is ultrabright gold without any sign of age. What you have lost is the original surface *and*, to a great extent, the intent of the framemaker. Yes, the surface can always be repatinated, but will never be equal to the original. It will always look like a regilded frame.

So if, in cleaning your frame, you find you are removing patination you wish to keep, you may have to lighten your touch. Frame conservation is now being given as much respect as painting conservation, which became a significant profession with the discovery that so many fine paintings were being ruined by overzealous cleaning at home. People were literally scrubbing their canvases—sometimes with potatoes, sometimes with scouring pads—to remove the old varnish. Cleaning always made the art look brighter, but homemade remedies and a heavy hand invariably destroyed the paint's vulnerable top layer. And it is not just misguided consumers who have damaged fine art. A great many poorly trained art conservators have been guilty of overcleaning paintings. It is the most dangerous thing they can do.

Here are other points to keep in mind while working on your frame:

- Always wear clean white cotton gloves. The acids that accumulate in the palms of your hands can damage gilded surfaces.
- Never attempt to clean a frame using a water-saturated cloth. It will make the gold leaf come off.
- If you do any touching up yourself, avoid using liquid gold paint over the real thing, which comes in ultrathin sheets. This gold paint will blacken with age.
- You can touch up areas where minor chipping has occurred by brushing on watercolors, hand-mixed to match.
- Never use touch-up crayons, such as those made for hiding scratches on furniture. As these and other wax-based materials never dry completely, it is almost impossible for whatever finish is applied to adhere properly.
- You can clean a plain carved-wood frame the same way you would a gilded one; just don't soak it. And, as with a gilded frame, confirm its quality with a museum curator before you even think of touching it.

If, during the cleaning process, you expose the gold leaf, you will have to *re*lacquer at some point, even though the color—the patination—has been lost. The beauty of what we are accustomed to seeing in an old frame is not what the frame looked like in the nineteenth century but what the nineteenth-century frame looks like now with the subtle patination that has taken place over the years. Sometimes frame artisans added color to the lacquer they applied—to tone down the gold, although the gold itself has always come in many subtly different colors. Depending on the type of alloy that is mixed with it—copper, silver, or tin, for example—gold can be shaded to pick up touches of green, red, or yellow. The colors vary somewhat from country to country. A German gold is warmer, slightly redder than an Italian gold; an English gold tends to be yellowish. And each gold ages differently, once again depending on the alloys that have gone into the mix. It has not been documented whether framemakers have always known what effect the aging process would have, but they seem to have had the process in mind when they worked.

Aesthetics played a big part in what they did; so did cost. The finer frames appear to have more layers of gold, and the layers were thicker in the nineteenth century than they are today. Gold was hand-beaten (ultimately, machine-beaten) into superthin squares called leaves. Layering the leaves eliminated the overlap marks that diminish the beauty of the surface. Today, to emulate a valuable nineteenth-century frame, I would have to apply three or four layers of gold leaf.

Patination is the end point of the aging process. On an old frame, patination is the result of dirt's settling into the cracks and crevices of the ornamentation as well as the lacquer's yellowing and absorbing dust, smoke, and other pollutants. Patination creates a sense of three-dimensionality that helps define and highlight many of the curved, sculptural details. It has the effect of creating shadows. At the time the old frames were crafted, this three-dimensionality was achieved by using both oil and water gilding—so that the inner surface was duller and darker than the brighter, more reflective outer surface.

It cannot be overemphasized that patination is crucial—to the way an antique frame looks and to the possibility of regilding it properly. Never give a frame to a restorer to regild without offering some guidance. Don't trust the artisan to know what it should look like unless there is at least one remaining patch of the patinated, gilded surface. If you have a frame that has been totally stripped of gold, try to find one like it—in your framer's own collection or, if possible, in a museum. Urge your framer to try and match the "model" frame; there is no way of knowing what to do otherwise. Even if only 2 percent of the original gilding remains, the intent—if not the actual color—will be evident. Whatever restoration you attempt should not "improve" the finish but simply return the frame to that degree of gilding. Not only will the finish be authentic; so will the intent. Further, the object will seem to "breathe" better; it will have more life.

Any frame crafted in the nineteenth or early twentieth century has its own particular sensibility. After all, there is a reason it was given a certain color, a specific look. For example, if the frame happened to have been finished in silver originally and there is only a little bit left, you may want to consider gilding the frame in white gold or re-silvering it.

Examination and Documentation

Before making a final decision on whether to restore your meticulously cleaned-up frame, take time to enjoy looking at it as an object. Remove the screw eyes and hanging wire. You will find that the moment you take off the hardware, the frame will become an aesthetic rather than a utilitarian object. Can you see which way it was meant to be hung? Vertically? Horizontally? It is important to know what the intention was, and this should be reflected in the way the screw eyes are positioned. If your frame has no hardware, you can tell how it was originally hung by the holes that remain in the back of the frame. With a nineteenth-century frame there is another possible clue to the way the frame was allowed to hang over time: the "maid's mark." That is the bottom frame element. It may be darker than the side and top elements because it was dusted more frequently, and vigorously, and more of the gold has been rubbed off by these repeated cleanings. If your frame's maid's mark is evident, you might want to turn the frame upside down so the darker element is now on top. Since the top of a frame is usually in shadow, the frame will look virtually renewed by this shift in position. One purpose of a gilded frame is to reflect light back onto the artwork; thus if the bottom of the frame is dark, one of the frame's functions has been nullified.

When the old hardware has been pulled off, screw a pair of D rings into the back of the frame, one on either side. D rings are small metal objects with either one or two holes and, predictably, a ring. Now find a section of blank wall and position two nails so you can hang your frame on the nails, using the D rings rather than the rabbet, or lip, of the frame. The lip is extremely thin and easily damaged, and there is an ever-present danger that the frame could slip off the nails. Hung, even temporarily, from D rings, which you can find in hardware or frame supply stores, your frame is ready for viewing. Step back. Hopefully, now that the clutter is gone the way of the ugly grime, the frame will seem even more attractive than you could have imagined.

Seize the moment and take stock of your purchase or discovery. First, note how the frame is joined. Is it a miter joint, where the molding strips come together at a forty-five-degree angle, or a butt joint whose angle is ninety degrees? Are there other types of special joining devices that you can see? If there are any old nails attached to the back of the frame, pull them out if you can see that they were placed there for hanging purposes and not to join frame elements. Old nails add further data to the frame's documentation, perhaps providing important additional clues to the age of the frame—they could be hand-forged nails, after all. New nails tell you that the frame may have changed hands recently or had a relatively new painting mounted in it.

In surveying the frame, note if the corners are loose and whether any structural reinforcement needs to be applied, such as the attachment of brass mending plates to the corners. But before doing any work on the frame, you will want to put down a large piece of bubble wrap or several layers of soft cloth on your work surface, then lay the frame facedown. You might want to apply mending plates as a temporary measure—until you put the frame in the hands of a competent restorer—but under no circumstances should you nail anything into your frame. The act of nailing produces vibrations that loosen the composition material and ornamentation and could be damaging to the wood substrate. Always use screws; you make their installation a little easier by starting the hole with an awl and applying a little bar soap (dry, not wet) to the threads so the screws become slippery. You want the installation to be easy, and at the same time you do not want to apply undue pressure to any of the frame elements.

Every collector should maintain complete documentation of the items accumulated—of artwork, to be sure, and certainly of frames. You will need this documentation for insurance purposes and also to support any inquiries you might want to make about the value of the frame. Be sure your documentation includes complete measurements—the width of the molding plus both the inside and outside measurements of the frame—along with photographs. Color photographs are preferable, but black-and-white are acceptable. Make sure to shoot both the front and back of the frame, and keep in mind that the documentation is clearer if done after the hardware has been removed.

Try to avoid using flash when you photograph; the glare from even a modestly reflective surface is likely to blur many of the details you will want to capture and record. My advice would be to use natural light and 400-speed film, without flash. In addition to an overall, be sure to shoot the corner detail, and if there is special ornamentation in the center of a frame element, shoot the center detail as well.

When photographing the back, be sure to do a close-up of the label, if your frame happens to have one. Also, you will want to protect that label by covering it with a strip of acetate held down with tape around the edges. If there are any drawn or carved inscriptions, you should make note of them. Your photographs will provide a useful personal record; they may also be important should a museum or gallery express a wish to borrow your frame for a frame exhibition. A set of pictures, rather than the frame itself, can be sent to curators for their consideration.

CHAPTER 13

Collectors and Collections

F EW of my clients would call themselves frame collectors. If they collect, it is because they have acquired artwork they feel deserve frames from a period that closely approximates the date of their art. Yet as they acquire paintings and drawings, they are building frame collections in spite of their intentions. Most of them refuse to own two frames that are exactly alike. They are interested in frame variety—and in a variety of colors, surfaces, and scale.

For most people who purchase antique frames, the artwork itself takes precedence, but it is the frame that gives the artwork the spiritual connectedness that collectors seek. It is the frame that brings them close to whatever relationship they wish to have with the art. A frame that works beautifully with a painting makes the viewing experience so much richer and more rewarding.

James Dicke, an art collector, has a keen interest in historical accuracy where frames are concerned:

> Some years ago, I bought a small painting by an American artist, Irving Ramsay Wiles, made about 1910. It needed cleaning, and it was mounted in a really terrible little frame, something that could have come from a dime store. I sent the painting to a conservator to have it cleaned, then decided that what the painting needed, to set it off properly, was something contemporary, probably in silver gilt. So I bought a contemporary silver gilt frame to put it in, and the painting looked worse than ever. "What have I done?" I wondered. I couldn't imagine where I

was going to hang it, so I put it in storage and almost forgot about it.

Subsequently, I read an article about what Eli Wilner was doing with period frames and how period frames were really a transforming element for art. Determined that my little painting would be an acid test of this idea, I went to the storeroom and got out my Irving Ramsay Wiles and stuck it under my arm the next time I traveled to New York from my home in New Bremen, Ohio. It was a small work, only about eight inches by ten.

I made an appointment to see Eli, who asked for a little time to do some research. When I saw him again, he made a proposal involving an absolutely appropriate period frame. I bought it immediately and asked him to mount the painting in it. What came back to me seemed a totally different painting; for the first time, I could really appreciate it and I knew exactly where I should hang it.

It's true what they say — that if you have one really good piece of art in your house, nothing else looks quite right. Well, that's true also of frames. Now it's impossible for me to look at a painting without judging, as part of the viewing experience, whether it's in the right kind of frame or not. In fact, I think even those artists who decide that their work should not be framed are really stating that they want the wall behind it to act as the frame. So in the larger sense, everything is framed.

My collection is mostly late-nineteenth and early-twentieth-century American art, and it's fairly eclectic — with everything from J. G. Brown in the 1860s to Fairfield Porter in the 1960s. Eventually I had most of my collection reframed. It hangs in my home and in my office; there are several hundred pieces, and as a result a lot of them hang gallery style.

The collection is ongoing, but this doesn't mean that when I buy something at auction I immediately decide to have it reframed. Sometimes the pieces are in wonderful period frames that just need to be cleaned or restored; sometimes I'll live with a painting for a while and think about it, perhaps do some research before I make a decision about reframing. The point is, I try to frame everything appropriately now.

Like James Dicke, Glen Foster is a collector who has become a stickler for historical correctness where frames are concerned:

> I think there is an awareness that a collector has that a period frame well married to a particular painting can enhance his or her enjoyment of that painting—and of a collection as a whole. My collection is almost entirely marine art of the nineteenth century; there is almost nothing from the twentieth century. The collection is installed in my home; there is very little of it that I don't hang on my walls. My intention is to both display and enjoy what I have. The only time any of the art is out of my home is when pieces are lent to a museum show from time to time. If I don't have space to hang a particular painting, that means I don't intend to keep it.
>
> My New York City apartment is fairly small, so there is a large number of paintings displayed in a relatively compact space. That means the paintings are hung salon style, some displayed above other paintings. Thus there are a number of paintings on any given wall, but they are hung in such a way that each painting has its own space and can be viewed as an individual object.
>
> We remodeled the apartment after acquiring it, and at that point determined exactly where every painting would go— based on what seemed an attractive separation. Then we wired the various areas with picture lights to illuminate the paintings—which means they are permanent. Moving paintings around would be quite difficult; instead, we tend to replace one painting with another.
>
> The collection is well developed and well defined by now. I've placed the paintings by specific artists in their own areas so they can be viewed as a collection of each artist's work. Virtually every painting has a nineteenth-century frame that is very close in date to when the painting itself was made. I have tried to acquire frames that are as pristine as possible. One reason for this is that, for me, it's not only the form of the frame but the texture and hue that are so important. Also, for me, the initial finish is key. You can repair a damaged frame, but I think it's virtually impossible to recreate the color and

patina that the frame originally had. So I make sure that the frames I buy are in sufficiently good shape to maintain their original feeling.

In many instances, however, repair work and alteration have been necessary. Because so many nineteenth-century frames were compo, even the best of them have suffered a little damage here and there. In the hands of a skilled craftsman, however, they can be restored in such a way that the eye can't really tell any work has been done. And many of my frames have had to be altered.

I think cutting frames down to size is a given; it's very, very difficult to find a frame that is exactly right for a painting and is

An arrangement of empty frames makes a compelling visual display. Here, American frames spanning the nineteenth and early twentieth centuries are featured in three dramatic clusters: heavily embellished frames plus simple carved and gilded examples.

also exactly the right size. On one occasion, the frame we found was perfect in style but slightly smaller than what we needed, so we had it expanded. But once you do that, you have a small section of frame that is not original, something we generally shy away from. Ninety-nine times out of a hundred, I would sooner shrink a frame rather than expand it.

I have frames that are signed, and many that have the original makers' labels on the back. But for most of my frames, it is the quality of the frame that counts most, as opposed to who actually designed and made the object. For me, there is tremendous excitement in finding the right frame, something that really complements a work of art. Thus the frame is important as an adjunct of the painting itself.

Justine Simoni is a different kind of collector. She owns a collection of masterpieces that are just frames. There are a few paintings that came with the frames, and she has kept them to show the interrelationships; there are also a few framed mirrors. Among her collection of examples dating from 1820 to 1950 there are perhaps a dozen European frames—Spanish, Italian, English, Viennese—which exist here as examples of the genesis of various American frame styles. From these examples, it is possible to see how American frame artisans looked at frames from different cultures and incorporated various elements to create unique forms. These influences can be seen in the vast number of period frames that Justine owns, and what she has assembled is probably the finest single collection of American frames in the world.

Justine views them as objects. She has, very poetically, compared her frames to vases, in that they too are created with a specific function in mind but can be admired on their own as objects. A frame, like a vase, is designed to receive something, yet it can have great relevance when denied that function.

I had never given any thought to period frames until I went to have a portrait framed and decided that a period frame would be appropriate for it. What I bought, from Eli Wilner—without ever visiting his gallery—was a simple gilded frame made some time after 1900. It was sculptural, with flowing, curving lines. Just right.

When I later visited the Wilner gallery, I was overwhelmed by the beauty of the frames I saw displayed there. I was moved by them and began to feel passionate about them — in that they must be preserved, that their beauty must be protected. But of course the only way to ensure that something is protected is to own it, so I sat down with Eli to plan a collection. What attracted me, beyond the beauty of each object, was the craftsmanship, for the men who worked with their hands to create these objects really did have pride of creation. That's one reason these frames have so much meaning for me.

In renovating my home in Pensacola, Florida, I have made room for most of my collection, though much of it will be made available to museums for shows and traveling exhibits. I am not a natural-born collector. I have never collected anything in a serious way until now, but I have always loved boxes and vessels of all kinds. So, why did I become a collector of period frames? The short answer: passion.

When Justine's home renovation was finished, I took a crew of four to Pensacola to install the frames. It would have been impossible to design the installation on paper; instead, we actually laid it out — outdoors under a roofed-over area that was kind of a carport. We would lay out a group on the ground, move them around until we were reasonably satisfied, then bring them into the house. We would hold them up, move them around and step back. Sometimes we made substitutions, but mostly we adjusted the positions until our visual judgment told us the arrangement was right. We worked wall by wall and room by room for a week until the layout was done. It took another week to complete the actual installation. The entire house was laid out before a single frame was hung.

Arranged on the floor, the frames looked beautiful, but when we hung them, the difference was incredible. They had no sense of weight anymore; even the biggest and heaviest of them seemed feather light. Raised from the floor and placed on the wall, they were elevated as objects. It was a transformation such as you might experience when placing a fine piece of sculpture on a pedestal. A frame actually elevates a painting just as a pedestal elevates a piece of sculpture.

The Simoni frames were arranged one inside the other, sometimes two on a wall, sometimes three. We grouped them not according to when they were made but according to aesthetics. Color and form guided us rather than accurate historical dating. Justine wanted the collection to look alive, as though it had always been there, so in terms of the way the paintings are grouped and hung, her collection relates more to each room, to the architecture of the spaces, and to the furnishings.

Justine's furniture is an interesting mix, though mostly American from different periods. Our frame choices were partly determined by each room's major pieces. For example, where there was a large, carved chest, we hung a Hermann Dudley Murphy that had similarly carved details right above it. Or because a fireplace had a screen decorated with vine motifs, we located a beautiful frame with tiny vines, little tendrils twisting out of the centers.

When furnishings and frames are paired this way, they really speak to each other. We tried to find elements in the frames that

In this grouping, a delicate frame of the 1850s made with applied composition ornament is surrounded by two masterfully carved and gilded Italian frames of the late nineteenth century.

caught some aspects of what was going on in a room. In effect, we considered each room and its furniture as art, and related our frames to this art just as you might relate these same aspects of a room to sculpture.

We worked in ten individual spaces in the house plus the bathrooms and entryways. Literally every room in the house has frames. There is one entryway where all the frames have a silvery tone. In another space there is a black and gold frame made in America that surrounds a black Spanish frame that surrounds a small Stanford White frame, which is very dark. The three work beautifully together. Each on its own is exemplary, but together they are exceptional. When hung perfectly, they enhance each other.

This enhancement impacts not only the way a work of art is perceived but its value as well. New York's two biggest art auction houses periodically borrow frames from my gallery to surround some of their paintings. These are two very bottom-line organizations, believe me; they don't borrow frames just for the sake of appearances. I think they feel that they can get much more for each painting put on the auction block if it has an appropriate frame. The frame enhances the presentation — it completes the "packaging" of the item — and the right frame puts the painting in context with its time. Where frames are concerned, I think historical accuracy is valid and valuable.

Since the 1980s, antique American frames have been elevated into the realm of art, taken seriously by collectors and curators throughout the country. Museums from coast to coast have been conducting exhibitions; many museums now label their frames as well as their paintings; and in 1997, a three-day symposium held at New York University focused exclusively on period frames. Where nineteenth-century American frames were once tossed out like refuse, they are now being saved and coveted. The result is that frame prices are escalating and the supply in the marketplace is dwindling. It's still possible to find labeled frames but harder than it ever was to find signed examples. And museums, art dealers, collectors, and institutions of every variety are expressing concern about the frames they own, caring for and cataloguing these objects.

At last, period frames have come into their own.

CHAPTER 14

The Miracle of Restoration

I have always been involved in frame restoration, for my own collection and for my gallery, but it has only been since 1989, when I established a separate restoration studio, that restoration services have become a major part of my business. It took a long time for interest in frames to reach the level wherein the public began to feel that restoration was necessary or important. For years I consigned work to a number of different artisans; then I decided I wanted to have a firmer grip on the quality of work being done and the pace of completion. I found space in Long Island City, in a two-thousand-square-foot building that had been a glass-cutting factory. Eventually our growth warranted moving a few blocks away to an eleven-thousand-square-foot space with facilities for frame storage plus elbow room for my staff of skilled gilders and carvers.

In an article published in the October-November 1992 issue of *Picture Framing Magazine,* Suzanne Smeaton sums up the restoration process this way:

> The two main components which require attention in the proper maintenance and conservation of period frames are the structural support (usually made of wood) and the surface decoration. Consolidation of the wood substructure generally involves rejoining open corners, repairing cracks and splits, and strengthening weakened areas. These repairs should be made with minimal change to the original appearance of the woodwork. It is important to preserve any evidence of the maker's marks, such as labels or inscribed identification. As in the study

of furniture, these elements provide documentation of a frame's design and construction.

Understandably, making structural repairs, however, important to the restoration process, is less demanding in terms of skill repertoire than making surface repairs. Indeed, the most painstaking aspect of restoring a frame is matching the gilded portions, because old gilding has a natural patina that is difficult to even attempt to match. It is much easier to restore pieces of carving that have come off; their replacements can be copied or cast from undamaged sections of the existing frame. Even so, only a qualified restorer should attempt to do this kind of work. It is not a job for the unschooled or inexperienced.

Casting with Rubber

For most surface restoration, we cast molds that are similar in concept to dental molds; they are made of the same rubber that is used in the preliminary stages of producing dentures. The rubber, malleable when it is at room temperature, picks up the subtleties of or-

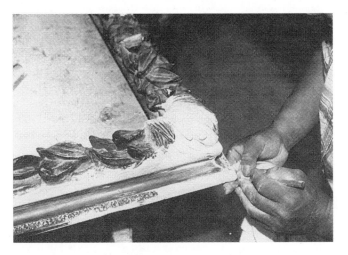

In the restoration studio, repaired ornament is rearticulated, or chased, to render crisp detailing.

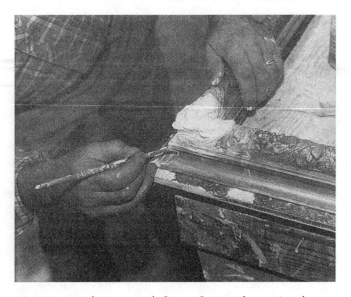

An artisan applies gesso to the damaged areas of an antique frame.

namentation design—every nuance, in fact. After taking an impression, we make a mold into which a plasterlike material is poured. It hardens as it dries, and is then removed from the mold.

Regilding a frame, or a section of a frame, is relatively inexpensive—at least in terms of the cost of materials. For a three-by-four-foot frame that is, let's say, five inches wide, the total cost of the gold would be about $300. But the amount of labor involved in the restoration work that precedes the gilding could add up to one hundred hours, perhaps as much as two hundred—at $75 to $100 an hour. Before making such an investment, you should know whether a frame is worthy of it.

When to Restore, When to Let Alone

I remember an instance when a prominent New York art dealer submitted a watercolor in a period frame that he wanted to have replaced. I examined the frame closely and concluded that there was no need to replace it; the frame was beautiful. It was filthy, however, and there were pieces missing that had broken off. I suggested that the frame be cleaned and then restored, rather than replaced. What convinced the dealer to let us do it? Removing the nameplate, which described the artwork and named the artist. When we got it off, we showed him that there was bright, glistening gold underneath, which suggested what the rest of the frame might potentially look like. In restoring it, we had to remove an encrustation of paint that had turned brown and, by then, was covered with grime. We stripped off the paint, and the gold was there. We felt we had saved something important.

To Restore or Let Alone?

Someone knowledgeable must make that determination, someone experienced in either frame or furniture restoration. There are many instances wherein frame restoration would not be worthy of the effort. If a frame could be replaced for $2,500, for example, why put $3,500 worth of restoration into it? In some cases restoring the

In restoring this frame, a whole new layer of gesso was first applied. So far, new gilding has been applied to only half of the re-gessoed surface.

frame could be important, no matter what its value—for example, if it is original to the painting it surrounds. Part of the determination must be based on whether the frame dates from the period when the artwork was produced, or if it is original to the painting, and certainly whether the art itself is important.

If, say, it's a frame made for a painting now worth $500,000, you will want to take care of that frame. Replacing it would alter the artist's idea of how the painting should be displayed. In the case of the watercolor sent to us for frame replacement, we did very little beyond cleaning the frame and removing the paint that obscured the gold. We restored some missing areas, but the pattern of orna-

Master gilder Jose Perez is shown applying gold leaf to the restored areas of this frame.

An agate stone is being used to burnish the newly gilded surface of a restored frame.

mentation had some abrasions where the blueness of the bole showed through, and the dealer opted to let such flaws remain.

Sometimes we are asked to work on a frame that is very dark, and we don't even clean it very thoroughly. We want it to remain dark. At the time the frame was made, perhaps it had a very bright surface, but its owner may be accustomed to the frame—a dull surface that makes a subtle complement to a painting—and prefer that it remain that way. Clearly, the look of years and years of accumulated grime works so well with the painting that we have no choice but to leave it alone; it has become part of the painting's character.

My particular view of frame restoration is that you do as little as you have to, and leave as much of the original as you can. If you start playing with certain surfaces, it's hard to know when to stop. You'll find a little damage here, a little damage there, and by the time you start laying on gold leaf in a finish that matches the old patina, you'll realize that you are redoing the entire frame. If the restoration work is done well, the value of the frame will not be diminished. What will be lost will not be monetary value, but history: contact with the old. A highly skilled frame restorer can make the new look old, often to the point of being able to fool a discerning eye, but the result is nothing more or less than an able simulation.

By the early 1990s, my restorers and I had learned to experiment successfully with a variety of surfaces. We had always been able to match gilding, but it wasn't until then that we were able to capture the feeling of a lacquered finish that had been confined to a smoke-filled room for more than a century, and the way that finish had absorbed accumulated pollution and dirt. Over the years we experimented with different types of paint, adding pigmentation to the otherwise translucent gel-like lacquer. It is truly amazing what can be done today.

To Restore or Not to Restore, and if So, How Much?

These are questions a professional must deal with, but the key to providing answers turns out to be yet another question: Is the frame suitable for use on a truly great painting? If a frame curator confirms that it is, then going the whole way with it is justified, whether you plan to use the frame by itself, with a mirror, or to surround a great painting of like vintage.

From time to time we have done complete frame restorations. For example, we redid the frame for Thomas Eakins's *The Swimming Hole* for the Amon Carter Museum in Fort Worth, Texas. The frame was almost completely painted over, so we stripped it down to the gesso and, while incising all of the detailing, uncovered one little speck of the original gilding. We found some gold that would match that speck, applied it, and the frame looked great.

Why did the museum ask us to go to so much trouble? Because the painting had been acquired for $10 million, and that was its original frame, probably chosen by Eakins himself. So the very thought of replacing it made no sense. How would you value a frame like that, one that the artist himself had chosen for one of his own great works? It would be impossible to assign monetary value to it when paired with the painting, but separate from the painting—on its own—it might bring $65,000 or more, an incredible amount when you consider that as recently as the early 1980s it would have been considered a $2,500 frame.

Cutting Down Old Frames

We have general rules regarding the cutting of old frames to fit certain paintings, but these "rules" are altered or broken nearly every time we go to work. Normally we would try to cut a frame at the corners, but each example presents a different challenge. Often, each element of a frame must be dealt with separately. And while I would normally insist that no signed frame should ever be cut — each is a work of art in its own right — there are always exceptions to be made.

For example, I acceded to a request to cut down a signed frame that was going to enclose Childe Hassam's *Room of Flowers*. The painting had sold at auction for $5.5 million, and the frame was one of my best Carrig-Rohane examples, but it was an inch and a half too big.

Because the painting had such value and this was the kind of frame such a painting would have had, it was worthwhile to have the frame cut down. The cut is virtually impossible to see. I was pleased to have done it, as Hermann Dudley Murphy, one of the Carrig-Rohane partners, had actually made frames for Childe Hassam's paintings, so there was a historical connection between framemaker and artist. Moreover, it was a perfect aesthetic pairing; the frame worked beautifully with *Room of Flowers*. I would not have cut that frame for just any painting — and never to fit a mirror or a particular space on a wall.

Beyond aesthetic considerations, there is usually a cost factor. Cutting a couple inches off of a three-by-five-foot frame could take fifty hours, depending on the type of work that must be done. So unless you have a frame that is an heirloom or has enormous value, you should think twice before investing money in cutting it down, or restoring it, for that matter. Sentimental value is another factor that often deserves consideration. I have known people who have spent a fortune on restoring the original frame that surrounded their grandmother's portrait. Neither the portrait nor the frame was worth very much, but when sentimental value is involved, you cannot attach dollar signs to it.

Here is something worth keeping in mind: When you have a frame cut down, be sure to keep the pieces that are removed. These are part of the history of the frame. Also, having them will enable you to make sure the restorer has matched the color perfectly when the restoration job is complete.

Frame Expansion

Generally it is much more difficult to expand a frame than to cut it down. With expansion, two or more new sections must be fabricated so that they will fit in perfectly and never be noticed. Depending on the complexity of the frame's design, you may have to expand two sections of each element. On an element that has a big center ornamentation, for example, you could certainly not cut right through the center; you would have to make cuts—and put in small extensions—on either side. An amazing amount of thought and work is involved, and you'll obviously want to do it right the first time.

What you are doing, in a sense, beyond resizing a frame, is trying to think the way the original frame artist did. You don't want to ruin his concept or compromise his design. Nor do you want to have to resurface the whole frame just because you are cutting or expanding it. So you have the double challenge of replicating ornament and matching finish.

Restoration Guidelines

Every frame has its own set of problems, and not all of them are easily anticipated. Take a relatively simple frame with no corner ornamentation: Logically it should be cut in the corners, if its size is to be reduced, but something so seemingly straightforward and simple could become incredibly time-intensive due to the fact that one or more elements may have become warped over time. When you cut it and try to rejoin it, you could be surprised to find that one side might be half an inch higher than the other. And to get the cut-down elements to work together harmoniously may take ten times longer than could have been imagined. The greatest risk, beyond the time and expense that may be involved, is that a less than skilled and experienced restorer will not know how to rectify the situation and may end up destroying the frame.

Whether you are expanding or reducing a frame, restoring or simply cleaning it, make sure you get a set price from the restorer you have chosen. Going in, you should know what the maximum price will be and have an ironclad assurance that this price will not be exceeded. If the person you are dealing with cannot make this declaration, you should talk to someone else. You don't want a time-and-materials arrangement—it's too open-ended.

A competent restorer should be able to examine a frame and do enough testing to know what the risks are and what the true scope of the work ultimately will be. If extra hours are required to complete the job, let him bear the brunt of it. Think what thirty extra hours could do to a budget!

One reason nineteenth-century frames were considered worthless and were so often thrown out is that they are so fragile. No one wanted to deal with them. Restoring a compo frame could be so time-consuming that, until recently, no one could justify putting money into it. Generally, carved-wood frames, being less fragile, are easier to work with, but restoring a carved frame can be difficult because there are so many flat planes where any and all surface problems—involving either color, detailing, or finish—seem magnified. With a compo frame, which is likely to be covered with so much more ornamentation, alterations are more easily hidden.

What makes old frames so extraordinary is that they are such delicate objects. And the fact that you can still find examples at flea markets—and own objects of such beauty that have survived for so many years—is altogether remarkable. Consider how easy it is to break them. Drop them or just knock them into a wall and they will shatter. If you get them wet or overheated, they will disintegrate. Millions of frames have been destroyed through the years; what we have left are miraculous survivors.

An art dealer I know, a man in his eighties who used to be a frame dealer, recalls a time in the 1940s when gold was in such short supply that old frames were being burned to melt down the gilding. The melted gold was sold, and the profits were divided among the dealers. I don't know how much gold a single frame yielded; I do know that frame dealers knowingly destroyed vast amounts of product—not eighteenth-century frames, of course, but those made in the nineteenth century. It was something akin to frame persecution that I don't think will ever happen again.

CHAPTER 15

Framing and Hanging Artwork

THE process begins with a drawing, print, poster, or stretched canvas — and ends with framed art that has been hung to enhance a wall or, indeed, an entire room.

Matting is used decoratively nowadays, picking up or complementing colors in a drawing or watercolor, but its primary purposes are to separate the art from its frame aesthetically and to protect works on paper from the glass. Sometimes the frame impacts too heavily on the work, in which case the mat eases a transition by providing a neutral border against the art.

In framing a work on paper, keep in mind that the art and the glass must never touch. With contact there is the certainty of moisture buildup, which will take the form of mildew spots that discolor the paper. The separation achieved by the mat creates a tiny space through which air can travel, discouraging moisture accumulation. When framing works on paper, be sure to consult an established, respected framing dealer or the conservator at a local museum to determine the appropriate matting procedure. I always rely on museum curators; they will never recommend framers who do not produce quality work routinely. Some museums even have up-to-date lists of recommended framers; a framer not on that list is not worth calling.

Glazing materials come in many forms for many different purposes. In addition to regular glass and Plexiglas, stocked by any frame dealer or studio, there is old glass, which many people covet for its imperfections; wavy surfaces and bubbles floating inside, for example. Although it *is* highly sought after, there is no way to assess its value, as there is no established market. However, there is a general awareness — an understanding, if you will — that old glass is important. So when searching for old frames, stay alert to the possibility of finding old glass as well; scour the stores and flea markets for it. People who love old prints, samplers, and folk art very often collect old glass. It will always have value. So, too, will these new glazing materials, each of which has a special purpose:

Den glass is coated with an antireflection film. When you are looking at a picture framed in this material, you won't see your own reflection. Nor will the glass reflect other objects in the room.

Protective Plexiglas will filter out more than 90 percent of the ultraviolet rays that strike it. Any work of art on paper is likely to fade under the punishing rays of sunlight, or any light, for that matter, that hits it directly. Be careful not to put any form of Plexiglas in direct contact with artwork made of pastels or loose charcoal. Plexi builds up static electricity that tends to pull these materials off the background material, transferring them from the paper onto the Plexi surface inside. Always use glass instead.

When fitting artwork into a frame, it is important to separate the art from the rabbet, that channel at a frame's inner edge into which the artwork fits. You can do this with a strip of felt secured with a nonacidic glue available from an art supply store. It will keep the rabbet's sharp edge from creasing the edge of a painted canvas, for example. Don't forget that, like paper, wood will burn. Separating frame and painting is like an additional ounce of protection. You should also make sure the painting rests in the frame securely. Any shifting around means additional unwanted friction that erodes the surface of the work.

Hardware

Always use brackets or picture hooks; don't just hammer nails into walls. And make sure the hardware will support weight that is heavier, rather than lighter, than your frame. Don't underaccessorize the hanging capacity of your frame. When installing a D ring, make a point of putting it into the outermost section of the frame; this is usually the thickest and strongest part. Be sure to note the thickness of the frame before putting screws in; you won't want to drive a hole all the way through the frame. Most important, you'll want to make sure the hardware can support the frame and what-

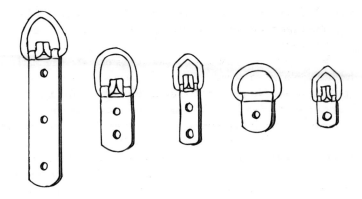

"D" Rings

ever you mount within it. Use four D-rings if you are unsure whether two or three will do. And always check the hardware yourself to make sure it is firm—even if the frame has been shipped to you by a gallery or dealer.

Siting

When choosing a site for your frame, avoid outside walls that lack proper insulation. Such walls are, to a degree, porous, which means that changes in temperature and humidity will affect the wall, and the frame and artwork as well. Try to avoid walls that are perennially cold and damp—or very warm and dry. No extreme is desirable. If your choices are limited, however, and the only possible site for a particular piece of framed art just happens to be a poorly insulated outside wall, there is a way to compensate: You can

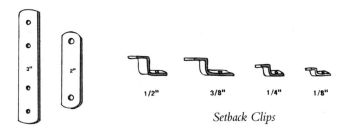

Setback Clips

Mending Plates

mount little spacer bars on the back of your frame so that air can circulate behind it modifying the extremes of heat and cold, dryness and dampness.

Before putting a hammer or drill to the wall, make sure the wall surface you have chosen does not shield plumbing pipes or electric wiring that could be punctured or otherwise damaged by the hanging process. If the surface of the wall is delicate or you want to give it an extra measure of protection, you may want to mount rubber bumpers where frame and wall will meet. Or, using acid-free glue, fasten felt to the back of the frame. You may feel a need to adjust the angle between the frame and the wall, particularly if the frame surrounds a mirror and you wish to control the image or light being reflected. A length of plastic bubble wrap rolled up, tubelike, and taped to either the upper or lower back of the frame will successfully tilt the frame up or down as needed.

Tools of the Trade

Professional picture installers regularly use just a few basic tools: hammer, screwdriver (to penetrate Sheetrock instead of a drill), three types of pliers (shown: flat-nosed pliers, bladed pliers,

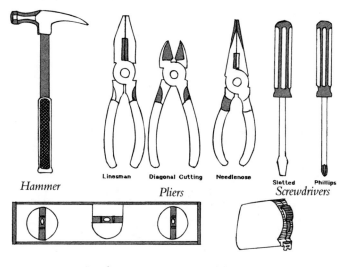

Hammer   Linesman   Diagonal Cutting   Needlenose   Slotted   Phillips

Pliers   *Screwdrivers*

Level   *Tape Measure*

and nail-pulling pliers), and an awl—to mark the spot for the drilling or nailing. As important as any of these implements to the framing process is a carpenter's level and a yardstick or tape measure.

For most hanging jobs, I recommend using commercial picture hooks. These come in three sizes: one-nail, two-nail, and three-nail hooks. The type you choose depends on the weight of the piece to be hung. These hooks are usually brass, and are affixed to the wall with a tempered-steel nail that makes a narrow hole in the plaster or Sheetrock it's angled into. If you are hanging a fairly heavy piece on a Sheetrocked wall, you will want to drill a hole and insert a toggle bolt. Once inside the wall, the toggle opens up; outside the wall, you put on a nut that you tighten against the toggle to make it very firm, but leave part of the bolt exposed—perhaps a quarter or three eighths of an inch—from which to suspend the frame.

For large, heavy pieces such as framed mirrors, what is known as reciprocating wood is often used. A strip of wood two or three feet long is cut lengthwise on an angle—say, forty-five degrees. One piece is applied to the wall, the other to the back of whatever you are hanging. On the wall side, the bevel is *away* from the wall; on the frame side, it should be *toward* the wall. If installed properly, the two sections will be joined so that one flat edge rests on another, holding the frame in place. Reciprocating wood is often used to hang cabinets as well as frames that are too fragile to risk focusing a lot of stress on just one area.

Keep in mind that picture hanging is a visual experience. You may wield a yardstick and level as skillfully as any professional, but if the ceiling sags a bit or the door or window moldings are not

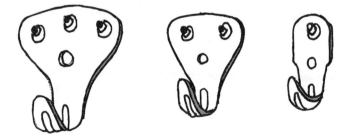

Picture Hooks

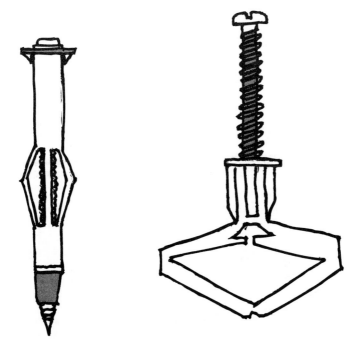

Toggle Bolts

plumb, even the most "level" installation is going to look skewed. What you need, in addition to a level, is a second pair of eyes for guidance or confirmation. If yours is the more discerning eye, let your partner hold the frame so *you* can step back to double-check its position. The human eye knows when a picture is straight.

Knurled Nail   *Eyehook*   *Molding Hook*

If the wall you are working on is not smooth or plumb or if it is wavy or bowed, there is more than one way to compensate. You could, for example, use wire loops to link the D rings on the back of your frame to the picture hooks. Or you could put up a hanging rod system, which is basically a narrow wood strip nailed to or hung from the ceiling. Hang your picture from wires suspended from brass molding rings or S-shaped hooks attached to the strip—just as you would suspend pictures or mirrors from old-fashioned picture molding.

When dealing with a normal, or routine, hanging situation, most pros prefer to work with two picture hooks instead of one, because of the shared weight distribution. Also, two hooks help a frame stay in place better, being less affected by dusting, jarring, or vibration. Some people like to hang pictures directly from the hardware screwed into the back of the frame, but using wire strung from one D ring to another is infinitely preferable, and the flexibility is greater. Here, step by step, is how you would hang framed art once the wire has been threaded on:

1. With help from your partner, hold the wire level against the wall in two spots—they could be six, ten, or twelve (or more) inches apart. That distance is called the spread; it marks how far apart your picture hangers should be. The larger a framed piece is, the longer your spread should be— ideally it will be at least half the width of the piece itself.

2. Let's say you decide you want a twelve-inch spread. You would hold the wire taut, pressed to the wall in places twelve inches apart. Then, using the tape measure, your partner should measure the distance from the bottom of the frame to that taut wire you are holding. Let's say that distance is twenty-four inches—make a notation indicating a twelve-inch spread that is twenty-four inches from the bottom of the frame.

3. Now hold the piece up for your partner to see, or have your partner hold the painting or mirror in this position so you can back off and look at it. Once it's in place, take another measurement: from the floor to the bottom of the frame. Say, for the sake of argument, the distance is fifty inches; adding the previous twenty-four to it will give you a height of seventy-four inches. Mark it.

4. At this point you should determine where you want to locate the center of the piece, and to do this you must be certain that its horizontal placement is correct. How far should it be from that adjacent wall on the right or that doorway on the left? Once you have equalized the measurements and "eyeballed" the position to confirm that it's right, mark it.

5. Next, draw a horizontal line at the seventy-four-inch level, and a vertical line (either real or imagined) from the spot that marks the center of your frame. Where the two lines intersect is where the hanging process will be focused. If you have decided on a twelve-inch spread, mark one spot six inches to the left of center, the other six inches to the right. If you want an eighteen-inch spread, measure nine inches in either direction, and so forth. The two spots you mark are where you will install picture hooks or drill holes to accommodate other types of hanging hardware.

If you are at all unsure about where to site your framed piece, before marking or otherwise defacing a wall, consider cutting a sheet of cardboard or brown wrapping paper the exact size of the piece and moving it about on the wall until its position pleases you. A template of this character will help you deal effectively with the spatial needs of the piece and suggest how it will relate to other objects in the room. But you won't know how well a piece of art actually works until you hang it and step back from it. Framed art in a room takes on characteristics no template ever could.

Storing Your Treasures

Frames, like many other collectibles, should not be acquired purely on the basis of where you might put them or what you might put *in* them. If you like them, you will be able to find a way to display them. And you can certainly rotate your collection. If, for example, you decide to hang one or more frames on the wall to be admired without artwork or mirrors, you might also decide at some point in the future to take them down, replacing them with paintings or prints for which you have equal affection. Fine-art collectors do this all the time. What counts here is how you treat your frames when they are off the wall.

The safest way to store them is to have a rack built so they can be standing up instead of lying down. They should never be stacked or leaned against one another or against a wall made of plaster, which could cause some of the gilding to rub off. An ideal frame rack looks like a storage cabinet for old LP records, except that the bottom of the rack has a scrap of carpeting stapled to it as cushioning. Frames standing in the rack should lean against sheets of stiff cardboard and not each other.

Never store frames in an attic, as it tends to be too dry, or a basement, which is usually damp. Frames should be accorded the same treatment as fine wood furniture. When you have to store them, a closet is the best location as long as you are certain a balance of dryness and dampness exists. Neither extreme is favorable, though dryness is the worst affliction, as it causes wood to contract. The damage caused by dry conditions depends on how much contraction, followed by expansion, occurs. When the wood contracts, the composition material on top of it will contract, and then expand, along with it. When shrinking takes place, the gesso under the composition material tends to squeeze up against itself. It remains that way until expansion takes place and cracks are formed because of the pressure, from below, on the composition material. Dryness itself is not damaging, only the expansion that sets in afterward.

It is understandable, then, that no frame should ever be hung or stored near a heater. On the other hand, a wood frame can certainly be hung in a bathroom if ventilation is good and you don't place the frame right beside the shower.

In a storage closet you might want to keep your frames out of harm's way—perhaps high up. A rack isn't essential here, as long as the frames are not stacked or leaned against one another on a shelf. An alternate solution would be a pair of two-by-fours extending out from the wall like sturdy hooks. Staple or glue strips of carpeting to the upper surface of each "hook" to create a soft bed to rest your frames on. Place sheets of cardboard between them so the frames do not touch.

If you need to ship a frame from the place of purchase or if you decide to send the frame to a museum or conservator for examination, you will need a wooden crate. It should be big enough so that there is a margin of two to three inches around the frame. Protect your frame by wrapping it first in glassine, a very thin tissue, then in bubble wrap. Damage occurs when a frame shifts, so make sure to pack it so there is no movement within the crate. But before packing it, make sure each section has been secured with the mending plates that are normally used to span or brace frame joints; you don't want one section to fall off and bang about inside the crate, damaging the surface. Mark the crate "Fragile" and choose a reputable carrier—trucking is safer than flying. In either case it's a good idea to wrap the crate in plastic and seal it, in case it should sit for a time on a loading platform or runway in the rain. Water will destroy a frame quicker than anything; the gesso will lift, as will the composition material. Best advice would be not to ship a frame by any means in adverse weather.

Creating a Collection

If you have a few old frames or have stumbled across some dust-encrusted examples up in the attic, you may find—once you have identified them and established their worth—that you like them a lot and, further, that you like the idea of owning them. Perhaps you'll want to build a collection. But before making further acquisitions, think about what attracts you to frames—just as you would if you were starting a collection of coins or porcelain animals.

Do you fancy their shapes, their profiles, their sculptural properties? Are you fascinated by frame ornamentation or by patination on the gilded surfaces? Would you prefer a collection that embraced the entire history of framemaking, or do you like focusing on one particular period? Do you want only American examples, only European or British, or a mix? To fully understand your taste, take time to look at frames.

Frame auctions are rare in the United States, but they take place regularly in major European cities. Domestically you will find antiques dealers for whom frames are a specialty—and a special love. Also a great many contemporary frame shops have old frames lying about. This is less likely now than in the 1970s, but it is possible. *Ask.* Tell the gallery owner of your interest in old frames. If he or she doesn't have any, there might be a good local source that you can be referred to. Thrift shops and flea markets are good sources because so many people continue to turn up old frames—in closets and attics—and, lacking interest, want to get rid of them. There are "finds" to be had here, just as there might be at antiques shows where a group of dealers are brought together in one space.

Always focus on the frame, not on the painting or mirror it surrounds. You might find a valuable mirror at an estate sale or an auction of old paintings—a frame even more valuable than the mirror being auctioned. Even if you don't bid or buy at such functions, *look*. Just looking will expand your perspective. And talk to museum curators; I can assure you that they will enjoy discussing antique frames.

Also, determine right away how much you can afford to spend. The size of your budget will help you determine what the nature of your collection should be. Depending on how affluent or committed you are, you won't necessarily buy ten or more frames at once. Chances are, each one will be a major purchase, made over time, and each acquisition will be a major challenge: to your vision, your judgment—your pocketbook, of course—and your connoisseurship.

Bibliography

Adair, William. *The Frame in America, 1700–1900.* Washington, D.C.: AIA Foundation, 1983.

Baird, Henry Carey. *The Painter, Gilder and Varnisher's Companion.* H. C. Baird and Co., Philadelphia. (Based on Watin, this book was reprinted throughout the nineteenth century.) *See also* Watin.

Baldwin, Charles C. *Stanford White.* New York: DeCapo Press, 1931.

Basso, Hamilton. "Profiles: A Glimpse of Heaven — II." *The New Yorker,* August 3, 1946.

Brangwen, Michele. "The Importance of Scale in Framing Art." *Picture Framing Magazine,* March 1995.

_____ "Always in the Frame: The Frames of William Merritt Chase," *Parrish Art Museum Journal,* Parrish Art Museum, Summer 1993.

Brettell, Richard R., and Starling, Steven. *The Art of the Edge: European Frames 1300–1900.* Chicago: The Art Institute of Chicago, 1986.

Burke, Doreen Bolger. "In Pursuit of Beauty." *Painters and Sculptors in a Decorative Age.* New York: Metropolitan Museum of Art, Rizzoli, 1986: 320–26.

Burns, Stanley. *Forgotten Marriage: The Painted Tintype & The Decorative Frame 1860–1910.* New York: Burns Press, 1995.

Cahn, Isabelle. *Cadres de Peintres.* Reunion Des Musees Nationaux: Hermann Editeurs Des Science et Des Arts, 1989.

_____ "Degas's Frames," *The Burlington Magazine,* April 1989.

Coburn, Frederick W. *Individual Treatment of the Picture Frame.* New York and London: International Studio, 1906: 12.

Coles, William A. *Hermann Dudley Murphy (1867–1945).* Exhibition catalog, New York: Graham Gallery, 1982.

Curry, David Park. *James McNeill Whistler at the Freer Gallery of Art.* Washington, D.C.: Freer Gallery of Art, Smithsonian Institution, in association with W.W. Norton & Co., New York and London: 1984.

Danly, Susan. *For Beauty and for Truth: the William and Abigail Gerdts Collection of American Still Life*: catalog by Susan Danly and Bruce Weber. The Trustees of Amherst College, Amherst, Massachusetts; 1998.

DeMazia, Violette. "What's in a Frame?" *Barnes Foundation Journal of the Art Department,* vol. 8, no. 2, Autumn 1977: 48–64.

Derby, Carol. "Charles Prendergast's Frames: Reuniting Design and Craftsmanship." *The Prendergasts & the Arts and Crafts Movement.* Williams College Museum of Art, 1988: 28–43.

Dolmetsch, Joan D. "Colonial America's Elegantly Framed Prints," *The Magazine Antiques,* May 1981: 1106–12.

Eastlake, Charles L. *Hints on Household Taste.* New York: Dover Publications, 1969.

Ferber, Linda and Gallati, Barbara Dayer. *Masters of Color and Light: Homer, Sargent, and the American Watercolor Movement.* Washington, D.C., and London: The Brooklyn Museum of Art in association with the Smithsonian Institution Press, 1998.

Gray, Nina. "Frame Choices of the French Impressionists." *Picture Framing Magazine,* May 1995.

_____ and Smeaton, Suzanne. "Within Gilded Borders: The Frames of Stanford White." *American Art.* National Museum of American Art: Smithsonian Institution, Spring 1993.

Greenthal, Kathryn. *Augustus Saint-Gaudens Master Sculptor.* New York: Metropolitan Museum of Art, 1985: 122–24.

Grieve, Alastair. "The Applied Art of D. G. Rossetti: 1. His Picture Frames." *The Burlington Magazine,* January 1973: 16–24.

Grimm, Claus. *The Book of Picture Frames.* New York: Abaris Books, 1981.

Haboldt & Co. *Portrait de L'Artiste: Images des Peintres 1600–1890.* Paris: 1991.

Hamlin, A.D.F. *A History of Ornament.* New York: Cooper Square Publishers, 1973.

Harris, Cyril. *Illustrated Dictionary of Historic Architecture.* New York: Dover Publications, 1977.

Harvey, Eleanor Jones. *The Painted Sketch: American Impressions From Nature 1830–1880.* Dallas, Texas: Dallas Museum of Art, 1998.

Harwood, Kathleen. "The Life of a Painting," *Trinity News,* Fall 1994.

Heckscher, Morrison H. *The Beekman Family Portraits and their Eighteenth-Century New York Frames.* Furniture History, 1990.

_____ and Bowman, Leslie Green. *American Rococo, 1750–1775.* New York: Abrams, 1992.

Heydenryk, Henry. *The Art and History of Frames.* New York: James H. Heineman, Inc., 1963.

_____ *The Right Frame.* New York: Lyons & Buford, 1964.

Hobbs, Susan. *The Art of Thomas Wilmer Dewing: Beauty Reconfigured.* Washington, D.C.: Smithsonian Institution Press, 1996: 83–85.

Hoenigswald, Ann. "Vincent van Gogh: His Frames and the Presentation of Paintings." *The Burlington Magazine,* vol. 130, no. 1022, May 1988.

Horowitz, Ira. "Whistler's Frames." *Art Journal #39,* Winter 1979–80: 124–31.

Jones, Harvey L. *Mathews. Masterpieces of the California Decorative Style.* Santa Barbara: Peregrine Smith, 1980.

Katlan, Alexander W. *American Artists' Materials Suppliers Directory—Nineteenth Century.* New Jersey: Noyes Press, 1987. Since 1990, Madison, Connecticut: Soundview Press.

_____ *American Artists' Materials Volume II: A Guide to the Stretchers, Panels, Millboards and Stencil Marks.* Madison, Connecticut: Sound View Press, 1992.

Latimer, Tirza. "The Total Picture." *Arts & Crafts Quarterly,* vol. 6, no. 3, 1995: 6–10.

MacTaggart, Peter and Ann. *Practical Gilding.* Welwyn, Herts, United Kingdom: Mac and Me, Ltd., 1984.

Mason, Pippa. *Designs for English Picture Frames.* London: Arnold Wiggins & Sons, Ltd., 1989.

_____ and Gregory, Michael. *Of Gilding.* London: Arnold Wiggins & Sons, Ltd., 1989.

Mendgen, Dr. Eva. "Painting and Frame in the Second Half of the 19th Century." *Der Kunsthandel-Europe.* Huthig: 36–41.

_____ *In Perfect Harmony: Picture and Frame.* Waanders, Vitgevers, Zwolle: Von Gogh Museum/Kuntsforum Wien, 1995.

Mills, Sally. "The Framemaker's Art in Early San Francisco." *Art of California.* November 1990, vol. 3, no. 6: 54–59.

Mitchell, Paul. "Wright's Picture Frames." *Wright of Derby.* London: Tate Gallery, 1990: 272–88.

_____ and Roberts, Lynn. *Frameworks: Form, Function & Ornament in European Portrait Frames.* London: Paul Mitchell in association with Merrell Holbertson, 1996.

_____ and Roberts, Lynn. *A History of European Picture Frames.* London: Paul Mitchell in association with Merrell Holberton, 1996.

Newberry, Timothy; Bisacca, George; and Kanter, Larry. *The Italian Renaissance Frame.* New York: Metropolitan Museum of Art, 1990.

Pederson, Roy. "Frederick Harer and the American Frame." *The Arts and Crafts Quarterly,* vol. 3, issue 1, 1989: 10–11.

Rebora, Carrie et al. *John Singleton Copley in America.* New York: Metropolitan Museum of Art, Abrams, 1995: 143–59.

Ring, Betty. "Check List of Looking Glass and Framemakers and Merchants Known by their Labels (before 1860)." *The Magazine Antiques,* May 1981: 1178–95.

Roberts, Lynn. "Nineteenth Century English Picture Frames." *The International Journal of Museum Management and Curatorship.* London: Butterworth & Co., Ltd, 1985: 155–72.

Roche, Serg; Courage, Germain; and Devinoy, Pierre, *Mirrors.* New York: Rizzoli, 1985.

Schiffer, Herbert F. *The Mirror Book.* Exton, Pennsylvania: Schiffer Publishing, Ltd., 1983.

Schiller, Joyce. "Frame Designs by Stanford White." *Bulletin of the Detroit Institute of Arts,* vol. 64, no. 1, 1988: 20–31.

Simon, Jacob. *The Art of the Picture Frame: Artists, Patrons and the Framing of Portraits in Britain.* London: National Portrait Gallery, 1996.

Smeaton, Suzanne and Gray, Nina. "Within Gilded Borders: The Frames of Stanford White." *American Art.* National Museum of American Art: Smithsonian Institution, Spring 1993.

_____ and Wilner, Eli. *The Art of the Frame: American Frames of the Arts and Crafts Period*. New York: Eli Wilner and Co. Inc., 1988.

_____ "Period Frames on Contemporary Paintings." *Picture Framing Magazine*, February 1996: 8–16.

_____ "A Perfect Marriage: Choosing the Right Frame for a Painting." *Picture Framing Magazine*, November 1994: 8–16.

_____ "European Antecedents to American Picture Frames." *Picture Framing Magazine*, September 1994: 34–39.

_____ "Modernist Frames." *Picture Framing Magazine*, May 1994: 10–14.

_____ "Reproductions or Exact Replica Frames?" *Picture Framing Magazine*, March 1994: 82–88.

_____ "19th Century Print and Drawing Frames." *Picture Framing Magazine*, December 1993: 6–10.

_____ "Like a Setting for a Jewel." *Picture Framing Magazine*, September 1993: 85–90.

_____ "Nineteenth and Early Twentieth Century Portrait Frames in America." *Picture Framing Magazine*, June 1993: 88–92.

_____ "Museums Redefine the Borders of Art." *Picture Framing Magazine*, March 1993: 59–64.

_____ "Fluted Cove Frames: America in the 1860s." *Picture Framing Magazine*, December 1992: 18–19.

_____ "Frame Restoration and Conservation." *Picture Framing Magazine*, December 1992: 77–84.

_____ "American Frames of the 1850s." *Picture Framing Magazine*, November 1992: 18–19.

_____ "The Reward for the Artist." *Picture Framing Magazine*, October 1992: 64–68.

_____ "Eastlake Style Picture Frames." *Picture Framing Magazine*, July 1992: 38–39.

_____ "The Frames of Frederick Harer." *Picture Framing Magazine*, March 1992: 60–61.

_____ "The Arts and Crafts Period." *Picture Framing Magazine*, October 1991: 90–92.

_____ "The Picture Frames of Charles Prendergast." *Picture Framing Magazine*, August 1991: 66–67.

_____ "The Frame Designs of Stanford White." *Picture Framing Magazine*, March 1991: 32–34.

_____ "Frames in Context." *Antiques and Fine Art*. January/February 1991, vol. 8, no. 2: 110–17.

_____ "Whistler Frames: An Extension of his Art." *Picture Framing Magazine,* November–December 1990: 36–37.

_____ "The Reward for the Artist." *Sanford Smith Beaux Arts Show Catalog March 1990.* New York: Sanford Smith, 1990: 8–10.

_____ "American Frames of the Arts and Crafts Period 1870–1920." *The Magazine Antiques.* November 1989: 1124–37.

Strickland, Peter L. "Documented Philadelphia Looking Glasses, 1800–1850." *The Magazine Antiques,* April 1976: 784–94.

Thornton, Jonathan. *Compo: The History and Technology of "Plastic" Compositions.* American Institute for Conservation Preprints, 1985.

Van Rees, Virginia. *The Historic American Gilded Picture Frame: Its Importance to the Appraiser.* Personal Property Journal, American Society of Appraisers, vol. 2, no. 3, Autumn 1989: 11–19.

Watin, M. *L'art du peintre, doreur, vernisseur.* Paris, 1744. *See also* Baird.

Wattenmaker, Richard J. *The Art of Charles Prendergast.* Greenwich, Connecticut: New York Graphic Society, 1968.

Wenzel, Paul and Krakow, Maurice. *Sketches and Designs by Stanford White.* New York: Architectural Book Publishing Company, 1920.

Wilner, Eli and Smeaton, Suzanne. *The Art of the Frame: American Frames of the Arts and Crafts Period.* New York: Eli Wilner and Co., Inc., 1988.

Video

Wilner, Eli and Co., Inc. *The Art of the Frame: American Frames 1820–1920.* New York: 1991. 18 min.

Wilner, Eli and Co., Inc. *Beyond Architecture: The Frame Designs of Stanford White.* New York: 1995. 36 min.

Index